FIRE ON PARLIAMENT HILL!

FIRE ON PARLIAMENT HILL!

Jane Varkaris & Lucile Finsten

THE BOSTON MILLS PRESS

Parliament Building on fire. The Standard, Montreal.
Courtesy Bibliothèque nationale du Québec.

Canadian Cataloguing in Publication Data

Varkaris, Jane, 1928-
    Fire on parliament hill!

Bibliography: p.
ISBN 0-919783-67-8

1. Parliament Buildings (Ottawa, Ont.)-Fire,
1916.*   2.   Fires-Ontario-Ottawa-History.
I.   Finsten, Lucile.   II.   Title.

FC3096.8.P37V37 1988   971.3′84   C88-093935-4
F1059.5.09V37 1988

Cover painting by Canadian Artist Henri Fabien, 1916.
    –Courtesy National Archives Canada, C11072.

Edited by Noel Hudson
Cover designed by Gill Stead
Typeset by Linotext, Toronto
Printed by Ampersand, Guelph

Published by:
THE BOSTON MILLS PRESS
132 Main Street
Erin, Ontario
N0B 1T0
(519) 833-2407
FAX 519-833-2195

ACKNOWLEDGEMENTS

The authors are indebted to Peter Robertson of the National Archives of Canada, whose exhibit of photographs related to the fire on Parliament Hill and entitled *"Aperçu: Phoenix on the Hill"* inspired the writing of this book. His kind co-operation in locating material related to the fire is gratefully acknowledged.

The help of Costas Varkaris, Cathie Milinkovich and Lawrence Finsten in the preparation of the manuscript is also greatly appreciated.

American Association
for State and Local History
Award of Merit

Winners of the
Heritage Canada
Communications Award

The Publisher wishes to acknowledge the financial assistance and encouragement of The Canada Council, the Ontario Arts Council and the Office of the Secretary of State.

TABLE OF CONTENTS

The Burning of the House of Assembly at Montreal, 25 April 1849. The Illustrated London News, 19 May 1849.　　　　　—Courtesy National Archives Canada, C2726.

INTRODUCTION

The choice of Ottawa as the location of Canada's capital was due in part to the willful destruction in 1849 of the House of Legislature situated in Montreal, which was the capital of the United Province of Canada from 3 November 1843. The Legislative building in Montreal was a large cut-stone structure and stood on ground later occupied by St. Ann's Market. On 25 April 1849, certainly not the proudest date in Canadian history, rioters, protesting against the passing of the Rebellion Losses Bill,* attacked Governor General Lord Elgin, broke windows and entered the building, overturning desks and smashing chandeliers. The House of Assembly was soon on fire. Because firemen were forcibly held back by the mob, the building was soon a mass of flames and very few items were saved.

Following this destruction, the capital city alternated between Toronto and Québec City. It was soon obvious that a permanent centre of the Legislature had to be chosen, and Kingston (the former capital for Upper Canada), Québec City, Montreal and Toronto clamoured for the honour.

So much dissension developed that Queen Victoria was asked to decide on the location of the capital city. Keeping in the mind the past trouble in Montreal and the proximity of Kingston and Toronto to the United States, a one-time enemy, the Queen selected Ottawa as the seat of the Legislature. She was guided by the advice of Governor General Sir Edmund Head, who considered not only the political advantages of the proximity of Ottawa to Canada East, but the fact that Ottawa had a magnificent location for capital buildings. On 31 December 1857, the Colonial Secretary informed the Governor General of the choice.

There was violent opposition in Parliament. Toronto and Québec City were favoured by the representatives for Canada West and Canada East respectively. However, neither would submit to a decision that would locate the capital in the other province. The issue revived bitterness between the two provinces, between Catholic and Protestant, and between English- and French-speaking people. The implementation of the Queen's decision was further delayed when the Assembly passed a resolution on 28 July 1858 "that it is the opinion of this House that the City of Ottawa ought not to be the permanent seat of Government for the Province." However, in February 1859, by a small majority, the Assembly affirmed the Queen's decision and Ottawa became the capital.

Wilfrid Eggleston, in his book, *The Queen's Choice*, considered that, although the question of "seat of Government" soured provincial politics for 20 years, "one important aftermath…was the government's determination to study the possibility of forming a federated union, so as to bring to an end the combination of weak ministries, bitter rivalries between Canada East and Canada West…and the persistent deadlock and impasse which had bedevilled the Province (of Canada)." However, in 1864 and again in 1866, the Fathers of Confederation were still debating the wisdom of making Ottawa the capital of the Dominion after Confederation.

---

*A bill to appropriate £90,000 for the losses suffered in Lower Canada during the Rebellion of 1837.

In 1859 a competition was held for a design of the proposed Parliament Buildings and was won by Architect Thomas Fuller, jointly with Chilion Jones. The style was twelfth-century Gothic. Thomas Fuller and Charles Baillargé (the latter soon resigned) were hired as architects and tendering procedures began for the construction of the building.

A ceremony took place for the breaking of the sod at 11 a.m. on 21 December 1859 and the first stone was laid on 26 April 1860. On 1 September 1860, as an important part of great festivities, the cornerstone of the building was laid by His Highness the Prince of Wales, later King Edward VII. The text of the cornerstone reflected that even at that late date the building was only "intended", and not necessarily firmly determined to be the seat of the Legislature of Canada.

The building, 472 feet long, was built of sandstone from a quarry in nearby Nepean Township. The arches over the windows and doors were warm-coloured red sandstone from Potsdam, New York, and the dressings were of grey Ohio freestone. The roofing was dark slate from Vermont decorated with a band of light-green slate from the same source.

In spite of the fact that the country was in the midst of the first Fenian raid, the new building was sufficiently completed in time to welcome the session of the Parliament of the United Province of Canada on 8 June 1866. When New Brunswick and Nova Scotia joined Canada East and Canada West to form the Confederation on 1 July 1867, Ottawa became the federal capital of the Dominion and the new Parliament Building became the home of the new Legislature. More chairs and desks for the members of Parliament were added and 194 hat boxes with locks were installed.

Nine years later, the Library of Parliament, also designed by Thomas Fuller, was officially opened with a grand ball given by the Governor General, Lord Dufferin, on 27 March 1876. Canada now had seven provinces to which the decorations of the Library testified.

Between 1876 and 1878, a great iron crown was added to the tower, increasing its height to 252 feet. By day, when Parliament was sitting, the Union Jack flag floated from the flagpole aloft the tower. By night, a cluster of lights on the crown informed the people that their representatives were still at work.

The installation in 1879 of the tower clock purchased from Messrs. Dent and Company, London, England, was the final step in the 20-year construction of the building. The total cost was $5 million. In addition to the rooms in the Centre Block, where the governing of Canada took place, there were suites of apartments for the Speakers of both Houses, the Gentleman Usher of the Black Rod of the Senate, and the Sergeant-at-Arms of the House of Commons. In 1905, Saskatchewan and Alberta joined Confederation and some of the needed space was provided by the addition of the West Wing in 1912.

For over 50 years, the Victoria Tower of the Parliament Building was an historic landmark attracting hundreds of thousands of visitors, who climbed the winding staircase to view from the great height the Ottawa River, the capital city and the Gatineau Hills beyond.

The Parliament Building without a crown just after Confederation.
—Courtesy National Archives Canada, C21954.

Library of Parliament and rear Centre Block. Photo by Samuel McLaughlin.

Centre Block of the Parliament Buildings (with crown) about 1880. Photo attributed to Samuel McLaughlin. —Courtesy National Archives Canada, C15106.

Interior of the House of Commons in 1880, length 88 feet and width 47 feet. Carpet and upholstering in green. Speaker's chair is on side. Photo by James Esson.
—Courtesy National Archives Canada, C 3874.

Interior of the Senate Chamber after 1882, length 88 feet and width 47 feet, carpeted and upholstered in red. Speaker's chair and throne are at north end. Photo by W.J. Topley. —Courtesy National Archives Canada, PA 8342.

GROUND FLOOR PLAN OF BURNED COMMONS

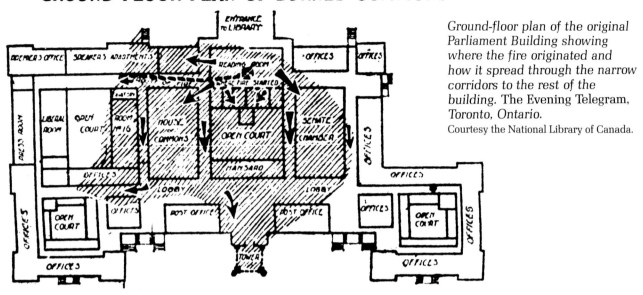

Ground-floor plan of the original Parliament Building showing where the fire originated and how it spread through the narrow corridors to the rest of the building. The Evening Telegram, Toronto, Ontario.
Courtesy the National Library of Canada.

HOUSE OF COMMONS
READING ROOM

Plan of the House of Commons Reading Room, from the Royal Commission Report of the Parliament fire. Rooms 28 to 33 are offices for some of the ministers.

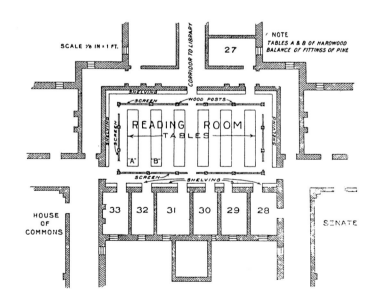

Chapter 1 — THE DISASTER

It was the clear, cold evening of 3 February 1916 and Canada's Parliament Building was being ravaged by fire. This magnificent structure, regarded by many to be one of the most beautiful of Gothic "piles" devoted to legislative purposes in the world, stood on the summit of Parliament Hill, which rises to a height of 150 feet from the edge of the Ottawa River. The Parliament Buildings were considered to be the crowning glory of Ottawa.

At 8:55 p.m., the fire began in the Reading Room of the House of Commons, a room 70 feet 7 inches in length by 36 feet 2 inches in width, situated between the House of Commons Chamber and the Library of Parliament.

The Reading Room contained six double reading desks, four of which were made of white pine, as were the ceiling, the walls and the shelving. The lower platform of the shelves held newspapers, which also covered the partitions on each side of the room. Around the room was a gallery with a large number of shelves where papers, newspapers and books were piled. According to later testimony, William Nickle* and Arthur De Witt Foster were in the Reading Room at about 8:30 p.m. and "conditions were normal."

Shortly before 9 p.m., Francis Glass was reading a newspaper. William B. Northrup had left minutes before. Although Mr. Glass was unaware of her presence, Mme Verville, wife of the Member for Maisonneuve, was also in the Reading Room when the fire started. Seeing the

flame, she quickly ran from the room, but was later unable to remember details of the incident.

Mr. Glass felt a current of hot air and turned around to see flames rising from the lower shelf of one of the desks. (Mr. Glass was sure that the fire started on the shelf under the first desk. Constable Moore and others were equally positive that it was the second desk.) Several similar fires*, the most recent two days before, had been easily extinguished and Mr. Glass was not worried. After looking in vain for Stanley S. Spencer, attendant on duty in the Reading Room, Mr. Glass quickly called for the Dominion constable, always on duty outside the Reading Room and one of at least seven policemen and plain-clothes men on duty at any one time in the Parliament Building. (Mr. Spencer was in the curator's room, having brought in a file of the Ottawa *Evening Citizen* newspapers.)

The fire was now burning rapidly above the desk and quickly consumed the newspapers upon it. Dominion Constable Thomas S. Moore, who had been on duty outside the Reading Room since 7:30 p.m., grabbed the fire extinguisher on the Senate side of the room and sprayed the

---

*See appendix A for listings of members of Parliament and Cabinet ministers.

*Between 1913 and 1916, thirteen fires were reported in Ottawa government buildings and extinguished by Dominion policemen. Of these, two fires occurred in the Centre Block. On 3 April 1915, a fire started in the sofa of Room 215. It was extinguished with one extinguisher. On 24 June 1915, a gasoline lamp exploded about 2:30 p.m. in a room used by electricians. This fire was extinguished with two chemical and one pyrene fire extinguishers. No record was kept of the number of fires that had occurred in the Reading Room. The fire closest in time to the February 3 fire was put out by W.G. Weichel and the caretaker on 26 January 1916.

chemical on the fire. Unfortunately the force of the spray spread the burning papers, igniting the material on the shelves and the partitions above. Although Constable Sergeant Edward Carroll, in charge of the police in the Parliament Building, and Constable C.E. Helmer used the hose that was stationed at the Speaker's door, they were compelled to abandon it, as the blaze and black smoke were already billowing out of the Reading Room door.

Of the incident, Constable Moore remembered "The fire fairly chased us." Recalling the small size of the fire when he first discovered it, Mr. Glass regretted not trying to deal with it himself. When he first saw the flame, he was sure it could be put out with a coat or doused with water from a five-gallon container that was sitting outside the door of the Reading Room.

Leaving the fighting of the fire to the constables, Francis Glass, Médéric Martin and Alfred Bradbury, brother of George Bradbury, rushed to warn other persons in the building of the impending danger.

The automatic fire alarm sounded in No. 8 fire station at 8:57 p.m. and within three minutes the firemen arrived at the fire. A second alarm sounded at 9:05 p.m. By this time, the fire had already broken through the roof and the House of Commons Chamber was ablaze. Under Fire Chief John W. Graham, the firefighters struggled to keep the fire from spreading, with particular attention to saving the Library of Parliament located behind the burning building. The fire doors between the Parliament Building and the Library were quickly closed by Mr. Connolly MacCormac, one of the librarians. A fire on the roof of the Library, discovered by Fire Chief Graham, was rapidly extinguished and, with the aid of the breeze which swept the fire southward, the Library was saved. During the night, showers of burning embers rained over the East Block, but firemen were able to keep the fire from spreading beyond the Centre Block.

At the time of the fire, Parliament was sitting and Deputy Speaker Edgar N. Rhodes, appointed only that morning, was in the chair. As always, the House of Commons mace was before him on the Clerk's table. About 20 members of Parliament were discussing ways to improve the marketing of fish in Canada, and William S. Loggie had just concluded his speech and was picking up his papers to leave. The door behind the Speaker's chair opened abruptly and members were warned that they must escape immediately. In various newspapers, Mr. Glass, Mr. Martin and Mr. Bradbury were each credited with carrying the news of the fire to the House of Commons. However, the Journal of the House of Commons (Hansard) officially recorded that at 9 p.m. M.C.R. Steward, Chief Doorkeeper for the House of Commons, broke into the room to announce, "There is a big fire in the Reading Room; everybody get out quickly." (He later wrote a letter of apology for breaking in so abruptly.) The Ottawa *Evening Journal* reported that Deputy Speaker Rhodes, "unceremoniously rose and walked quietly out of the Chamber."

The fire in the Reading Room was now racing along the corridors, fed by the freshly shellacked floors and highly varnished interior. With a roar, a tongue of flame broke into the House of Commons Chamber. Hon. E.L. Patenaude and others dashed out of the room toward the main entrance. William Loggie, Edward Nesbitt and several other members reached the door of the Chamber located opposite Room 16 (Conservative

"Photo taken at 10 p.m. Thursday night while the fire was burning fiercely." Toronto World.

—Courtesy the National Library of Canada.

headquarters), but the door was locked. Mr. Nesbitt broke the glass, cutting his hand, but the smoke poured in and they stumbled back through the desks to reach the main door. George Elliott yelled for the members to join hands. Michael Clark, E. Nesbitt, O.E. Turgeon and J. Douglas were among the last to leave the Chamber and they all suffered from smoke inhalation. Mr. Loggie was barely conscious when pulled into the main corridor.

Mr. Clarence Jameson heard a loud noise in the north end of the corridor. He was thrown as far as the glass door and was one of the last to escape the area, with singed eyebrows and mustache. In the struggle to escape the fire, Fleming Blanchard McCurdy, John G. Turriff, Hon. Frank Oliver and John James Carrick were slightly injured, but did not require hospitalization.

In the Chamber, Mr. M. Clark was knocked down by the force from a hose stream and was almost overcome by smoke. He emerged from the Chamber on his hands and knees. The Prime Minister, the Rt. Hon. Robert L. Borden, was at the main entrance and heard Mr. Clark "roaring like a bull" and shouting that others were in the Chamber and Visitors' Gallery. Fortunately, all those in the Chamber were safe. Hon. John Douglas Hazen, after finding the side door of the Chamber locked, made a dash for the door behind the Speaker's chair, racing through the smoke and flames. It would have been certain death to have turned back. He was slightly injured, but was able to accompany the Prime Minister in his survey of the devastation.

On that evening of 3 February 1916, Sir Robert Borden had remained in the House of Commons until about 8:40 p.m. He went to his suite located in the new West Wing and called his secretary, J. Boyce, to deal with his correspondence. One of the House messengers warned him of the fire and the pressing need to escape. Without pausing to get hat or coat, and avoiding the smoke-filled corridors, the two ran down the messengers' stairway to the vestibule. Fifty years later, in 1966, Frank Clarke, page-boy from 1911 to 1918, recalled that the Prime Minister proceeded to the vestibule practically on his hands and knees to avoid the clouds of smoke, hatless and coatless and with a white handkerchief over his face.

"Parliament Building on Fire before the Crown Fell." This picture appeared in several newspapers, including the Victoria Daily Times.

Courtesy the National Library of Canada.

Centre Block on fire at 12:30 a.m., 4 February 1916. Photo by J.B. Reid.

Courtesy National Archives Canada, C 10079.

Mr. James Morris loaned Sir Robert Borden his fur-lined coat and an attendant gave him a hat. Mr. Boyce was sent to the Prime Minister's residence for a hat, coat and overshoes. After presiding over the extraordinary meeting of the Ministers' Council, held later that night in the Chateau Laurier Hotel, the Prime Minister, before going home, walked through the crowd on the Hill and around the burning building.

When Mr. Martin and Mr. Glass shouted their warnings at the outset of the fire, Constable Paul Miller was on duty at the Visitors' Gallery door. He urged Mr. E.M. Macdonald, his friends and a few others in the Gallery to leave. Although they were unable to get hats or coats, people rushed without panic from the Gallery to the front of the building and outside to safety.

Equally fortunate was William A. Charlton, who was in Room 115 with Edmond Proulx. As smoke prevented their descending the winding stairs opposite the room, they went to the West Wing, where they were able to go down to the messengers' room and make their way to the vestibule and outside.

After warning people in the House of Commons and in Room 16, the Conservative headquarters, Mr. Martin, then Mayor of Montreal, rushed to the Chateau Laurier, where he put in a hasty call to the Montreal Fire Department. A special train of firefighters and equipment, including a motor hose engine, was put in readiness to leave for Ottawa. When at 11:30 p.m. he realized that little could be done to save the building, the order to leave was countermanded. However, the fire chief was asked to be ready to leave if the need arose.

Major Gerald V. White, who was in uniform, also rushed to Room 16 to assist the older members. He then helped in the work of rescuing several people trapped in the upper rooms of the southwest wing. Also in Room 16 were D.C. Ross and Alfred Bradbury, a stockbroker from Ottawa who helped the Hon. David Henderson to escape. In a very short time the window became the only way to safety. Michael Steele, John H. Fisher and Colonel James Arthurs, unable to wait for ladders, were forced to jump into a snowbank. Fortunately they were not seriously injured.

As the last members of the House of Commons made their escape, the glass roof shattered to the floor and the flames leaped skyward 50 feet. The fire rushed along the front of the building toward the Senate Chamber, which fortunately was empty, as the Senate was not sitting that evening.

Near the Senate Chamber, Colonel John A. Currie organized several members of Parliament and police into a fire brigade and they laid hose from the emergency supply in the corridor. They were able to arrest, for a short time, the complete destruction of the Senate Chamber, allowing some of its historic relics to be saved. When the lights went out at 10:30 p.m., candles and lanterns were found, but were not needed, as an abundance of light was provided by the flaming oak door at the west end of the Gallery and the quickly spreading fire. Finally forced to leave, those who were offering assistance regretfully closed the Senate Chamber door.

Although the members in the House of Commons had a narrow escape, in some cases the rescue of those who were elsewhere in the building was more dramatic. Dr. Edward L. Cash and Mr. MacNutt were in the lavatory, unaware of the fire. When they opened the door they were faced with a mass of flames. Seizing towels, they made a rope and threw it out of the window. Dr. Cash went down first, falling the last 20 feet. One of the caretakers joined Mr. MacNutt and lowered the ladder into the window well outside. Mr. MacNutt descended into six inches of water in the courtyard and the caretaker followed.

Of the members who were in their offices adjacent to the Reading Room, the Hon. Martin Burrell sustained the most serious injuries. When he opened the door of his office he was confronted with flames and smoke in the corridor. Seeing no avenue of escape, he ran through the inferno into the arms of the Hon. R. Rogers and the Hon. P.E. Blondin. The Hon. Burrell received serious burns to his head and hands. In the messengers' quarters he was attended by Dr. William Chisholm and Dr. Dugald Stewart, both members of Parliament. Seconds after the Hon. Burrell's escape, the Hon. Sir W.T. White tried to leave by the same door but was driven back by smoke. He and the Hon. C.J. Doherty, who were with the Hon. John D. Reid in his office, escaped by way of the Senate Chamber.

A story in Toronto's *Saturday Night* described the experience of Mr. Michel Siméon Delisle, who was in the barbershop directly under the Reading Room when the fire occurred: "A tongue of smoke darted through the ceiling and the barber's hand trembled, but being a thrifty man and anxious to get his money's worth, Delisle said, 'There's no hurry. Give me a close shave.' A lance of fire made a slash at him and the barber fled. Delisle got his close shave alright, but he got it getting out of the building. He said afterwards that he wasn't as addicted to close shaves as he thought he was." He was slightly injured during his flight.

Also able to flee from the basement through the dense smoke were Mr. E.L. Horwood, architect for the Department of Public Works, and Colonel Henry Smith, Sergeant-at-Arms, who was in the Clerk's office getting some papers.

Mr. A.K. Maclean was in the Chamber when the alarm was given and was one of the last to leave, exiting through the southwest corner. He went up to the third floor to warn the Nova Scotia members in Room 302. He joined Angus A. McLean and William F. Kay as they rushed down the stairs, but they became confused and separated. Mr. Maclean, unable to see where he was because of the dense smoke, ended up in the basement, where a policeman directed him out. Near the elevator, he found Mr. Kay, almost overcome with smoke, and helped him to reach safety.

Mr. John Stanfield, Member of Parliament and Chief Conservative Whip, Wilfrid Larose of the Hansard staff and George Simpson, Steward at the House of Commons, and his family escaped from their rooms by means of ladders extended to them by firemen. The Simpson family lost all their household effects. A.J. McMillan, caretaker of Room 16, was also rescued from an upper floor by a ladder put to him by Sergeant Carroll.

Although it was not recorded where they were when fire broke out, a number of members of Parliament were listed in newspapers as being slightly injured: i.e. Ernest Lapointe, William M. Martin and Pius Michaud. Mr. William F. Cockshutt burned his cheek, but was more concerned about losing the souvenir cane that had recently been presented to him.

There was concern for the safety of Joseph O. Lavallée, Member of Parliament for Bellechasse, who had not been seen since the morning of February 3. It was with great relief that it was learned that he had taken a train to Montreal that day.

Although not in the Parliament Building when the fire started, the Hon. Sir Sam Hughes, Minister of Militia and Defence, and his men played an important role on the evening of 3 February 1916. Major-General Hughes was enjoying an informal supper at the Chateau Laurier. Upon hearing of the seriousness of the fire, he immediately called out the troops of the local 77th battalion under Colonel Street and asked for the engineers also stationed at the Exhibition Building. About 70 soldiers came to the Hill. Quickly a cordon of troops was formed around the burning structure to hold back the crowds. The troops also assisted the firemen and policemen and took part in the salvage and rescue operations during the night. Conveyances of the Red Cross were requisitioned by the Department of Militia and Defence, and many loads of valuables were removed for safekeeping.

On one of the many rescues, the Hon. Hughes and his men hoisted scaling ladders and brought down the employees of the Parliamentary Restaurant, located in the west wing of the building. During their efforts, several soldiers were injured. Lieutenant Jack Hammel and Lieutenant McDonnell sustained head injuries from falls on the ice that quickly formed when tons of water from firemen's hoses froze in the frigid air. Others taken to the hospital were "Sapper" G. Clarke, Pte. Larocque, Pte. Collyer and Pte. Henry Dumoulin. Two soldiers were cut by falling glass. In spite of the intense heat generated by the raging fire, the icy wind rapidly chilled the soldiers and many suffered from frozen hands and faces.

Although not on the Hill at the time the fire started, the Duke of Connaught, Governor General of Canada, and the Leader of the Opposition, the Rt. Hon. Sir Wilfrid Laurier, rushed to the scene as soon as word of the fire reached them. The Governor General drove from his official residence and was forced to watch the destruction of the building for which his brother, Edward VII, then Prince of Wales, had laid the cornerstone in 1860. The Rt. Hon. Sir Wilfrid Laurier was at a concert at the Russell Theatre. As he drove up in his car, the roof of the House of Commons fell in and flames roared skyward. By the time they arrived, a tremendous crowd was gathering on the icy roads, though soon held back by the soldiers of the 77th Battalion and policemen. Sparks Street was congested with autos, hacks, streetcars and crowds of pedestrians. Throngs of people gathered in hotel lobbies asking about members of Parliament and friends. Restaurants close to the Hill remained open to accommodate the crowd.

In the early hours of the morning, three field stations were set up on Parliament Hill by the Laurentian Chapter of the Daughters of the Empire. These supplied the soldiers and workers with hot coffee and soup. Also, the soldiers' club on Wellington Street was kept open day and night providing soup and sandwiches and a place to get warm.

It is impossible to estimate the number of lives saved by the quick action of the building staff. Fred Wilson, Government Superintendent in charge of rewiring, and S. Marshall, contractor, went down to the basement at 10:30 p.m. because the lights had gone off, and within ten minutes, the switch which sent light to many parts of the building was tripped, facilitating the escape of many persons. Especially brave was Thomas Wensley, Chief Engineer, who was on the top floor of the building when the alarm sounded. Fearing there might be explosions in the boiler

One of Sir Sam Hughes' field kitchens at work serving coffee and soup to militia and fire workers. The Standard, Montreal. Courtesy Bibliothèque nationale du Québec.

room, he rushed down to shut off the steam. He escaped with a bruised forehead, having run into a pillar in the dense smoke.

The breeze that blew southward and helped save the Library of Parliament from flames hurried the spread of the fire to the Victoria Tower. The firemen directed on the tower thousands of tons of water, which then flowed down the concrete steps, transforming them into cataracts. By 11 p.m. the fire began its ascent of the tower, lighting window after window with its insidious flames as it raced from floor to floor. It engulfed the winding staircase that had carried hundreds of thousands of visitors to the lookout above and shot toward the crown, the streams of water falling far too short. The ring of lights on the crown flickered and, for the last time, went dark.

In his memoirs, Prime Minister Sir Robert Borden noted that while the fire raged, the tower clock struck the hours of 9, 10 and 11 o'clock, but was unable to fully strike the midnight hour. At its last knell, the bell crashed down into the depths of the tower. The clock mechanism faltered at 12:30 a.m. and the hands stopped.

The collapse of the crown, taken from the rear of the building, showing the Reading Room windows and the chimney tower on the left. The photographer was making a time exposure and shut off just as the crown fell. Picture in various newspapers, including the Halifax *Herald.*

Courtesy the National Library of Canada.

Finally, at 1:21 a.m. on the morning of Friday, February 4, the crown of the famous tower collapsed. The flagstaff remained up until the last, its gilt ball gleaming at its top. The fire was finally brought under control shortly after 2 a.m., but flared up again about 10 a.m. in the rear of the East Wing; a stone tower toppled outward, barely missing firemen and soldiers. One of the soldiers considered his escape, "a narrow squeak."

The fire continued to smoulder under streams of water continuously directed by the fire brigade, and there was further excitement about 8 p.m. on Saturday, February 5, when a report circulated that the East Block was on fire. Although the alarm was sounded from the East Block, the fresh outbreak was on the Senate side of the main building, where a draft from a dumbwaiter had fanned a flame from the smouldering embers. This last flame was quickly extinguished.

Also in the Parliament Building were members of the press. Seldom are newsmen and journalists present at unexpected events of such national importance as the devastation by fire of the Parliament Building. Instead of reporting a rather mundane debate on the marketing of fish, they were able to send to their home papers news of one of the most spectacular and tragic events in the history of the Dominion.

In the press gallery were Arthur R. Ford of the Toronto *News* and William Wallis of the Toronto *Mail and Empire*. Mr. Ford rushed to the press room to warn those finishing their reports that the place was on fire. H.F. Gadsby, a newspaper man, and Arthur Hannay of the Ottawa *Free Press* were there. As reported in the Ottawa *Evening Journal*, "Newspaper men are proverbially skeptical and just smiled at the warning. It dawned on them that there was a story elsewhere as they watched Ford stuff papers into his pockets." They made their escape from the press room, some men dropping 18 feet through windows to a snowbank below.

Albert Carle, parliamentary representative for *Le Réveil* and *Le Droit* was also in the press gallery. He ran to the press room for his coat. Upon leaving, he and his secretary were forced to crawl on hands and knees, directed by a policeman shouting, "This way." *The Evening Citizen* representative alighted from the elevator and was met by clouds of smoke. He raced outside. It was the elevator's last trip.

Because the event was unique in the history of journalism, so were the stories. The newsmen co-operated in sending bulletins, which were dashed off and delivered by messenger to the telegraph office and then to many destinations around the world. In the newsroom of the home papers, these bulletins were seized by skilful writers and elaborated into long, thrilling stories that were read at the breakfast and dinner tables of the world the next day.

As the few pictures taken during the night of the fire were sent by train and some time elapsed before they reached newspaper offices, the papers improvised in a number of ways. *The Montreal Star* and the Halifax *Herald* provided their readers with a picture of the smouldering ruins drawn from the description sent by telegraph.

When the pictures of the actual ruins arrived at the newspaper offices, the newsmen were delighted with the accuracy of the drawn picture. (See p. 29 for photo of ruins. Another night shot was retouched to make the effect of the fire appear more spectacular. For true picture, see p. 17)

Scene at the Parliament Building fire just after daylight, 4 February 1916. Firemen and soldiers hose the east wing of the building. The walls are crusted with ice. The Toronto World.

Courtesy the National Library of Canada.

Fire-gutted Centre Block still smouldering on the morning of February 4. Photo by John Boyd.
Courtesy National Archives Canada, RD 243.

Firemen fought valiantly but icy wind turned jets of water to ice. Photo by W.J. Topley.

Top: *Parliament from east side at dawn, February 4. New York Times.*

Bottom: *Ruins with ice on Centre Block.*

Courtesy National Archives Canada, C 38768.

Ruins on Friday morning at 11:00 a.m.   Courtesy National Archives Canada, C 42925.

Top: *A view of the Parliament Building, retouched.* The Evening Telegram, *Toronto.*

Bottom: *Picture of ruins from a telegraphed description.* The Halifax Herald.

Other newspapers took existing photographs of the Parliament Building from their files and sketched clouds of smoke and tongues of flame on the night sky to simulate the fire. (See title page for the spectacular results.)

Two Winnipeg papers published the same picture. *The Manitoba Free Press* added curls of smoke and clouds to portray a fire scene, whereas the Winnipeg *Telegram* published the picture without embellishment.

The burning of the Parliament Building continued to dominate the Canadian news for four or five days, but was quickly pushed aside by news of the war.

A number of eyewitnesses have written about the fire, certainly one of Canada's most historic conflagrations. One of the most poignant reactions was recorded by Canadian poet Duncan Campbell Scott, who wrote in a letter a few days after the fire that, though the fire was "terrible and tragic, it was the most terrifying and beautiful sight" he had ever seen.

Top: *The Parliament Building, Friday morning. The Winnipeg* Telegram

Bottom: *The Parliament Building on Friday morning, retouched.* The Manitoba Free Press.
Courtesy the National Library of Canada.

31

Mme Louis Morin.

Randolph Fanning

Bowman B. Law.

Mme H.A. Bray.

M. J.B. René Laplante.

Alphonse Desjardins.
(Steamfitter)

32 (No photo available for A. Desjardins, policeman.)

Chapter 2 — LOSS OF LIFE

The fire not only destroyed one of the most beautiful structures in Ottawa, but cost the lives of a number of Canadians. The following persons lost their lives in the Centre Block fire that fateful day: Mme Henri (Florence) Bray; Mme Louis (Mable) Morin; Constable Alphonse Desjardins, Dominion Police Force; Alphonse Desjardins, steamfitter, Department of Public Works; Randolph Fanning, Post Office Department; J.B. René Laplante, Assistant Clerk, House of Commons; Bowman B. Law, Member of Parliament for Yarmouth, Nova Scotia.

Due to the tireless efforts of policemen, soldiers, firemen and the Parliamentary staff, many lives were saved. However, it was with great sadness that the deaths of two ladies were announced. Mme H.A. Bray of Montreal, Mme Louis Morin of St. Joseph-de-Beauce and Mme Henri Dussault of Québec City had been for several days guests of Mme Albert Sévigny, wife of the Speaker of the House of Commons, and Mme Morin expected to return home on Friday. When the alarm sounded, the ladies were in the parlour of the apartment reserved for the family of the Speaker of the House. One of the ladies was playing the piano.

When the fire was discovered, Albert Sévigny raced upstairs from his office, where he was dictating letters. He yelled a warning and rushed to rescue his children. He grabbed Madeleine, five years old, and one of the nurses carried the ten-month-old baby. Nurse Bélanger was cut by flying glass. Mme Sévigny followed Nurse Tremblay, with the ladies behind her until they reached the first landing. Here, one of the ladies said,

"Wait a minute. Let's get our furs." Mme Sévigny tried to stop them, but the ladies went back upstairs. After leaving his daughter in safety, M. Sévigny tried to climb back up the stairs but was driven back by fire and smoke at the first landing. He fell and was helped out by a fireman.

Fireman Charles McCarthy and fireman Frank Schoener, driver of the fire chief, climbed a ladder to the Speaker's apartment in an attempt to rescue the ladies. Charles McCarthy, overcome by smoke, almost plunged headfirst through a window in the attempt. Fireman Schoener grabbed McCarthy and carried him down the ladder. He was taken to St. Luke's Hospital. Fireman Schoener returned with fireman Omer Daoust, found Mme Bray and Mme Morin and carried them down the ladder.

When the firemen reached Mme Bray and Mme Morin, they were found face down on the floor at the end of the corridor, hands clasped around their heads, hair scorched and garments considerably burned. No sign of life was evident. After being brought down the ladder, Miss Piper, a nurse, several doctors and a city policeman, using one of the Ottawa Electric Company pulmonators, tried to revive them, but there was no hope. Mme Sévigny kept repeating, "Oh, if only these ladies had only followed me instead of returning for their furs, they would have been safe." Mme Morin, about 30, left her husband and five children, from one to eight years of age. Mme Bray, 27, left her husband and a three-year-old boy. On February 17, at the request of her husband, Coroner Craig presided at an inquest into the death of Mme Mable Morin. The report

*Firemen hose the rear of the Reading Room and the passageway to the Library.
The area to the right of the Reading Room is where the ladies died. Photo by
John Boyd.* Courtesy National Archives Canada, RD 228.

of February 23 established that she died of suffocation due to smoke inhalation.

The third guest, Mme Dussault, fortunately escaped. She made her way to the master bedroom of the Speaker's apartment and, to escape the suffocating smoke, climbed out of the window and hung suspended from the window sill for ten minutes. She was encouraged by M. Sévigny, who was standing below the window, to wait until the firemen's net arrived. With smoke pouring out of the window behind her, she leaped 40 feet into the net. On learning that Mme Bray and Mme Morin were not behind her, she collapsed.

When the House met, the Rt. Hon. Sir Wilfrid Laurier, in a very emotional speech, said, "And what have we to say of the loss of those two young ladies, young, happy mothers, full of life, full of contentment, and appreciating the benefit of their station, visiting old friends in their present high station, and now no more."

After the fire was extinguished, Fire Chief Graham organized 25 men to clean debris and recover bodies. A second group relieved them and they worked uninterrupted until all the bodies were recovered.

Of the seven people who lost their lives in the fire, one was a policeman named Alphonse Desjardins and three were government employees: R. Fanning, Post Office Department; Alphonse Desjardins, steamfitter and uncle of the policeman of the same name; Jean Baptiste René Laplante, Assistant Clerk of the House of Commons.

Alphonse Desjardins, steamfitter, had safely escaped the burning building when he remembered his much-prized fur hat. Having retrieved it, he went to help Plainclothes man James E. Knox who, with Randolph Fanning and Alphonse

Desjardins, policeman, were directing a stream from one of the stand pipes in the basement of the Speaker of the Senate's apartment. Shortly after 12 a.m., Plainclothes man Knox ran a few feet down the corridor to straighten a hose. He heard a crash and the great ventilation tower above the corridor had collapsed. He was able to escape but the others were caught under the falling wall.

Alphonse Desjardins had been on the Dominion police force for five years, was married and had several children. His body was recovered on the

A search party in the ruins. London Illustrated News.
Courtesy the National Library of Canada.

evening of 6 February 1916. The two other bodies buried under the falling tower were recovered 7 February. When found, Alphonse Desjardins, steamfitter, was holding his hat. He was mourned by his wife Exilda, two sons, Horace and Lucien and his daughter, Colombe. Of the employees who perished, Prime Minister Borden said, "They lost their lives in the discharge of their duty."

The death of René Laplante, Assistant Clerk of the House of Commons, was also unfortunate. When the alarm sounded, he rushed up to his apartment on the second floor, near the suite used by Deputy Speaker Rhodes. Apparently, upon trying to leave, he became confused in the blinding smoke. Walter Hill, private steward to the Deputy Speaker, who, until that time was unaware of the fire, heard a noise outside his room and quickly pulled M. Laplante inside. Knowing their only escape was through the window, Walter Hill tore down the drapes, knotted them together and extended them from the window. M. Laplante was too afraid to leave by the window. Mr. Hill implored him to escape and left only when the heat became too intense. When Mr. Hill climbed out of the window, M. Laplante was on his knees praying and cried out, "For God's sake send someone back for me." Mr. Hill, who dropped about 20 feet to the ground from the end of the curtains, was knocked unconscious. He revived after some time in the hospital. M. Laplante's remains were found in a badly burned condition on Saturday, February 5.

As tribute to M. Laplante, the Prime Minister said, " It is not too much to say that the House of Commons never had a more capable, more industrious or more faithful officer...His death is an almost irreparable loss to the effective organization and work of the House."

The fact that many members of Parliament might have perished in so devastating a fire gave little comfort to those who mourned the death of a fellow member of Parliament, neighbour and friend, Mr. Bowman Brown Law, Member of Parliament for Yarmouth, Nova Scotia, who had left the House of Commons Chamber to make a long-distance phone call in the booth halfway down the stairs from the Commons' west corridor to the basement. From there he had gone to his office on the top floor of the building and had apparently tried to reach his locker but was unable to escape. On February 23, the remains of B.B. Law were found near his locker between the Reading Room and the House of Commons. His body was almost totally consumed except for a thigh bone and a few smaller bones. The remains were sent to Yarmouth for burial.

Mr. Law received many tributes, among which were those from:

Prime Minister Borden, "He was a man of kindly and generous disposition and of indefatigable industry in connection with all his public duties. He was always listened to with attention and respect when he rose to address the House."

Sir Wilfrid Laurier, "He has been for nearly twenty years a faithful servant of the House of Commons—a man whose courtesy, ability, activity and kindness every Member has learned to appreciate."

The Hon. Rodolphe Lemieux, "I am sure when it came to the time to go down into the valley of the shadow and meet the King of Terrors, he did so with that confidence which is given only to men who have lived as Bowman lived."

ERECTED TO THE
MEMORY
OF
BOWMAN BROWN LAW M.P.
REPRESENTATIVE OF THE
COUNTY OF YARMOUTH, N.S.
○   ○   ○
WHO MET HIS DEATH IN
THE GREAT FIRE
WHICH DESTROYED THE
PARLIAMENT BUILDINGS,
3RD FEBRUARY 1916

REQUIESCAT IN PACE

IN ADDITION TO MR. B.B. LAW, M.P. THE FOLLOWING
INDIVIDUALS PERISHED IN THE GREAT FIRE OF 1916:
MRS. FLORENCE BRAY, VISITOR
MR. A. DESJARDINS, DOMINION POLICE FORCE
MR. ALPHONSE DESJARDINS, PUBLIC WORKS DEPARTMENT
MR. RANDOLPH FANNING, POST OFFICE DEPARTMENT
MR. J.B.R. LAPLANTE, ASSISTANT CLERK, HOUSE OF COMMONS
MRS. MABEL MORIN, VISITOR

OUTRE LE DÉPUTÉ B.B. LAW, LES PERSONNES SUIVANTES
ONT PERDU LA VIE DANS LE GRAND INCENDIE DE 1916:
MME. FLORENCE BRAY, VISITEUSE
M. A. DESJARDINS, DE LA POLICE FÉDÉRALE
M. ALPHONSE DESJARDINS, DU MINISTÈRE DES TRAVAUX PUBLICS
M. RANDOLPH FANNING, DU MINISTÈRE DES POSTES
M. J.B.R. LAPLANTE, GREFFIER ADJOINT DE LA CHAMBRE DES COMMUNES
MME. MABEL MORIN, VISITEUSE

To honour the other individuals who lost their lives in the great fire, a commemorative plaque was unveiled on 3 February 1988 in the Hall of Honour. Courtesy Andy Shott.

A plaque in memory of B.B. Law, M.P. was mounted on the wall of the Hall of Honour in the new Parliament Building.

Statue of Sir John A. Macdonald and some salvaged furniture from the Speaker's apartment. The Standard, Montreal. Courtesy Bibliothèque nationale du Québec.

Chapter 3 — THE AFTERMATH

When dawn broke on Friday, 4 February 1916, firemen were still playing streams of water on the Parliament Building, deluging the area with tons of water. In the frigid air, giant icicles had formed on the remaining walls, and inside stalactites of ice hung on twisted pipes and girders. The frozen spray had turned the nearby statue of Sir John A. Macdonald a ghostly white.

On a horse-driven sled, a life-size portrait of a former Prime Minister was propped up, its frame blackened with smoke and coated with ice, the name obscured. Other salvaged portraits were being dug out of the ice and snow. The transportation of rescued artifacts went on all day.

Firemen worked continuously to find bodies of those who perished, and staff was hired to assess the material losses. All were thankful that the Library of Parliament was saved due to the alertness of Mr. Connolly MacCormac, a librarian, who is credited with closing the iron fire doors that separated the Library from the rest of the structure.

Firemen hosed the domed roof while soldiers helped to remove a large number of volumes which were taken by military motor lorry to government storage. All such books were returned to the Library by February 13. Although many volumes first thought lost were later found to be safe, many others were seriously damaged or destroyed by water. At one point on the night of the fire, six inches of water covered the Library floor. Fortunately, this floor was almost waterproof, a fact that saved the material stored below. The fire in the Reading Room destroyed an extensive collection of rare editions of the Bible; a valuable collection of ecclesiastical literature and law covering more than a century; hundreds of volumes of the Edinburgh Review, Quarterly Reviews and other periodicals, some dating back to 1807; some valuable scientific encyclopaedias and French-language dictionaries. All newspapers and files in the Reading Room were consumed. Particularly regretted was the loss of old newspapers, some of which were a hundred years old, including the prized first copy of La Minerve, published in Québec. However, as they were stored in the Library, the "live" newspaper files, which were bound, were saved.

A.E. Horton, Clerk of Journals and Proceedings, was able to save scrolls from the beginning of the session and the minute book of the printing committee. He carried them with him when he escaped out the window. However, lost in the Journal Room were all sessional papers for the last 10 to 13 years, petitions presented for the current session and Clerk's scrolls from the previous years.

J.P. Foley, Clerk of the Crown in Chancery, was driven back by the flames before being able to save the records dating back to 1841, which gave full details of all elections since that time. J.G. Pigeon reported that all Parliament reports and official documents in French "fell prey to the flames". All the important papers in the law clerk's office were destroyed.

However, many records were not lost. The fire spared the Prime Minister's office in the West Wing, which had been built more recently and proved to be more fire resistant. All his papers were found untouched, as were his hat and coat.

In the days following the fire, scorched official documents were picked up in parts of the city as far as a quarter mile away from the Parliament Building. One such report was from the 1896 period, notifying the Speaker of the House that the Clerk had been unable to locate Mr. Powell (then a member of Parliament), who was to be confined to the tower for some now unknown reason!

As in the Reading Room, everything in the House of Commons Chamber was burned. Certainly the article most mourned was the House of Commons mace, which is the visible symbol of power of the representatives of the people and is placed before the Speaker when Parliament is in session. This mace had a colourful history. It was used in Parliament when Montreal was the capital of the United Province. It had escaped the 1849 fire of the Legislative Building in Montreal.

Several versions of the story exist regarding its rescue, depending on the writer's loyalties. The Standard, Montreal, published what they considered to be the most accurate account. Apparently, one of the rioters seized the mace from the table, ran with it up to the dais, on which stood the Speaker's chair, and shouted, "I dissolve this House." He then attempted to march out of the building with it over his shoulder. The Sergeant-at-Arms chased him, grabbing the crown of the mace. Two rioters struck the Sergeant-at-Arms, one with the handle of an axe, and he was forced to relinquish his hold. Flames drove everyone out and the mace disappeared in the confusion.

According to The Standard, the mace was found the following morning on the porch of a boarding house where several members of the Assembly lived while Parliament was in session. The mace was turned over to Sir Allan MacNab, then leader of the high Tory Wing of the Opposition and in the 1850s the first British Prime Minister of "Canada." The mace was "somewhat bent and otherwise injured whilst in the hands of the mob." One solid-gold acorn was lost from the wreath of oak leaves and acorns that decorated the head of the mace, and the missing acorn was later replaced.

However, in the Parliament Building fire of 1916, fate was not so kind. When the ruins cooled, all that was found of the mace were several balls of gold and silver. Upon hearing of the loss, Colonel Sir Charles Wakefield, who was the Lord Mayor of London, and the Sheriffs of the City of London offered, through Sir George Perley, the High Commissioner for Canada in London, to replace it. A new mace which incorporated fragments of the old mace was fashioned by the Goldsmiths' and Silversmiths' Company of Regent Street, London, England, and was an exact replica of the old mace. An editorial appeared in the Winnipeg Free Press: "Thus, so to speak, the rebuilt Ship of State will sail on and on with the old binnacle refurbished and in place...."

On 28 March 1917, at the Guildhall in London, the new mace was presented to the Rt. Hon. Sir Robert Borden.

In February 1916, Sir Robert Borden had received a letter from Sophia Mary, the Duchess of Albemarle. The Duchess, who was the second daughter of Sir Allan N. MacNab, mentioned above, expressed sympathy to the Prime Minister and to the people of Canada on the loss of the building and the House of Commons mace. She recalled the story of the recovery of the mace after the riots of 1849 in Montreal and asked Sir

The new House of Commons mace.
Courtesy National Archives Canada, C 5850.

Robert Borden to give her a small relic of the mace melted in the fire of 1916. The Prime Minister arranged through Sir George Perley for her to receive a small piece "in memory of the association of her family with the history and life of this Dominion." On May 7, she sent a letter to Sir Robert Borden acknowledging its receipt and expressing her delight. She planned to take it to Sir Cecil Smith at the Victoria and Albert Museum for advice on how to have it mounted with an appropriate inscription.

Although on the night of the fire smoke from the corridors poured into the Senate Chamber, fire did not reach it until about 10:30 p.m. From the time that the fire alarm sounded, Senate messengers M. Gilman and W.D. Perkins, with Albert Low, John Currie, A. Hamlyn Ford, Chief Clerk of the Library of Parliament, soldiers and others worked frantically to save what they could. The Senate mace was carried to safety by police, with an escort of soldiers, and taken to a vault of the Dominion police.

A large portrait of young Queen Victoria painted by English artist John Partridge was saved with the help of Constable La Rose and A.H. Todd, a member of the staff, whose uncle Alpheus Todd, then the Assistant Librarian to the Legislative Assembly, had saved the same portrait in the 1849 Montreal Parliament Building fire. Both times the portrait was hastily cut from its frame to permit it to pass through a door. For many years the portrait, reframed after 1849, hung on the south wall of the Chamber of the House of Commons. When the Chambers of the Houses of

41

The second storey overlooking the Senate Chamber. London Illustrated News. Courtesy the National Library of Canada.

Furniture removed from the burning building. Photo by John Boyd.
Courtesy National Archives Canada, RD 244.

Parliament were redecorated, the picture was moved to the Senate Chamber, where it was hanging on 3 February 1916. The portrait, again reframed, now hangs in the Senate foyer of the present Parliament Building.

Another picture was removed from its frame during the rescue: the portrait of Speaker Power broke when physical force was needed to tear the portrait off the wall. Among those saved were two pictures, of King George III and Queen Charlotte, attributed to the English painter Sir Joshua Reynolds. Lost were the portrait of King Edward VII and Queen Alexandra and the portrait of King George V and Queen Mary.

Albert Low helped carry the Speaker's chair from the Chamber and a number of Senators' chairs were also removed, along with the brass ornaments from the Clerk's table.

The helpers raced to the rooms of the Speaker of the Senate and Mme Landry, who were in Québec City at the time of the fire. Mr. Ash and Mr. Wood, who were members of the staff of the Parliament Buildings, had made arrangements for removing silver and other valuables. Senator Lougheed and the Senate staff broke open desks and cabinets and removed all their contents. Pictures, furniture and trunks of personal belongings were rescued.

On the morning of Friday, February 4, there sat a little pile of goods near the ruins of the Speaker's apartment: a roll-top desk, a few chairs, books, and an 8-day clock that had stopped at 11:02. A soldier mounted guard. Also behind the Library, a pile of valuable books was covered with a tarpaulin, and there again a soldier mounted guard.

Lt. Col. Ernest J. Chambers, Gentleman Usher of the Black Rod, with a heavy heart, helped in the rescue operations. He finally had to abandon all hope of saving the uniform and the Black Rod itself, perhaps the oldest piece of Canadian Parliamentary regalia. It had been carried by successive Gentlemen Ushers of the Black Rod since the formation of Upper and Lower Canada. In 1898, Hon. J.D. Edgar, in his book, *Canada and its Capital*, describes its function, "When the representative of our Queen comes down in State to the Senate and desires to inform the faithful Commons of weighty matters, it is not at all surprising that she sends the Gentleman Usher of the Black Rod from the Senate to rap three times at the door of the Commons' chamber and, when admitted, to demand their attention in the Upper House."

Many of the rooms in the Parliament Building not gutted by fire were damaged by water. Arthur Hawkes, a writer who visited the Parliament ruins on 7 February 1916, described what he saw and his reactions in a lengthy article published in *The Standard*, Montreal. Following are excerpts from his descriptive and emotional article.

Destruction may leave beauty in its train, even as there is majesty in death, It breaks your heart to venture into the place where the House of Commons has been changed into heaps of rubble. As you turn from what was once a corridor and is now a heap of plaster and broken stone and look back to the entrance hall that has echoed the walking of every great servant of Canada since the Dominion was born, you glimpse sunshine through a little door...lentled in ice.... In the House, where panes of glass had been in the upper frame there (are) now portieres of icicles turned and twisted in the blast...a ghastly holocaust of architecture....

The entrance hall was lighted by two glorious electroliers. One on the side of the Senate lies tilted and broken on the floor. Its fellow is still intact but dressed in icicles.... Past where the post office was, your rubbers splash in pools upon the tesselated floor.

The telegraph rooms are gutted but, except for the unaccustomed water, the press room is undamaged by fire. The veneer on many pieces of furniture is lifting and curling. Near the typewriter, in need of a thaw, was an article, "The Sincerity of Parliament" awaiting revision.... The fire had done infinitely more to revise the sincerity of Parliament than anything a half-articulate writer could perform, be his pruning pencil ever so sharp.... On the desk...there was a tiny paper-covered volume of unconscious humour from Cape Breton whose gems even yet may be handed to a larger world.... A carpenter is chiselling ice out of the frame of an open window through which a laggard penman sought salvation....

Outside Sir Wilfrid Laurier's office, Guigere's [sic] room is a mess. The roll-top desk is smashed in and ice and charcoal abound. The clock upon the wall is burned and broken and tells twenty-one minutes to nine. In Sir Wilfrid Laurier's office, all the furniture is gone. The floor is covered with three-quarters of an inch of yellow ice and knobs of discoloured material—icicles the wrong way up. An ice

Corridor leading from Senate Chamber to House of Commons Chamber. The Standard, Montreal.

Courtesy Bibliothèque nationale du Québec.

encrusted cuspidor remains.... On the floor by the cupboard, a volume leans against a door embedded in an inch of ice through which the title page is clear, "The Many-Mansioned House and Other Poems," by Edward William Thomson. It is the only poetry of the ice age you have seen, and for a moment you understand the passion which makes a souvenir hunter out of a human being....

On the walls down which the water has streamed, three pictures remain — a photograph of Mr. Asquith behind where Sir Wilfrid used to sit; one of Lloyd George on the western wall; and a water colour scene....

From Sir Wilfrid's to Sir Robert's room is the whole length of the western corridor. On the way are rooms of the Liberal whips and the general rooms of Liberal Members...soaked and sorry-looking but otherwise unimpaired. The premier's room...was dirty and wet but not disastrously so..... Nothing was gone except papers which are not for the curious to see. On the desk was a copy of *Le Réveil*.

You turn eastward, into the Corridor of Death. The iron elevator on the right had a filigree of ice on the middle of its door like a crystal nosegay. It was the common access to the restaurant two floors above which was undestroyed.... Images of Macdonald, Mackenzie and others still hang on the wall, puzzled, maybe, by all the fluster and smoke.... It is not the unseen pictures that possess your mind. The ice has begun to attack your nerves....

Through an empty window you saw the littered courtyard and gutted walls of Room 16, and in the light beyond, walls forlorn and wretched and distorted columns sprinkled with snow.... You would fain turn back to escape closer acquaintance with so much desolation, but there is a fascination in the ruin of noble structures and you go ahead to see the worst....

In the Speaker's apartment you see broken and damaged furniture, the same which you admired when Dr. Sévigny lately called in the gallery for a social hour. The corridor...which his procession traversed four times a day is filled at this end as it is the other, with everything that comes to earth when walls collapse that were filled with pipes for water, pipes for gas and pipes for electrical wires....The second door to the Speaker's apartment is open and more dishevelled beauty is scattered upon the charcoaled and sodden carpet....

You cannot make the corridor to Room 16 or to the Reading Room.... The stairway to the basement is filled with stone, brick, plaster and iron. The crash that broke floors and twisted beams of iron left unharmed a mirror on the wall, a reminder that Death pays strange respect to fragile things. At the foot of those stairs, they yesterday found the body of a man, eager to defeat the flames before the enemy smote him. Somewhere, within fifteen feet of you two other corpses reposed....

(Beyond) the corridor the floor had vanished.... A stately passageway had become a pit. It yawns at you because they dug so much away to find the first corpse of the five men that were lost.... Here the double row of lockers began— pine boxes that had been dried and varnished for half a century, perfect preparation for a fire....

To find the spot from which to view the Chamber site, you must wiggle around a trembling wall. If this is the House of Commons that you see, it is verily a House not made with hands. It was thrown together by a Fiend. Remember what it was and whom it held and if you can stand unshaken here upon this smouldering mound and hear the moan of yesterday as it steals around these gaunt and blackened pillars, you are made of tougher clay than is commonly transformed to flesh and blood.

This was the House of Commons when the Prime Minister was a little school boy and when Sir Wilfrid was making the ends of law and journalism meet in Arthabaskaville.... Within these battered walls and upon this floor which is now dishonoured by tons of wreckage, most of the statesmanship of and a little of the folly of Canada has been expressed....

Everything they knew is gone. Where the Speaker ruled, the steps which the pages sat eager to do his bidding, the floor on which one Premier after another, and leader of the opposition succeeded leader, is a pit half filled with stone and soaked dust and twisted strands of wire, sprinkled with a light snow, as if Heaven, rushing to screen it from our mortal gaze, had given up the toll and turned away its face. In the hole lies the crumpled Mace covered with the ashes of the chair in which the Deputy Speaker spent his first and last hour of presidency here....

The tiers of desks behind which Members slammed their approval of friends and growled defiance to their foe, have vanished in blaze and smoke. The flat roof of oak and stained glass...came down to mingle with the flaming floor. Pointing straight to where the Speaker sat, there are a dozen plumber's pipes looking for all the world like so many machine guns trained upon the spot where, more than all others, the dignity of speech, free and unafraid, was vindicated and acerbity of controversy assuaged....

A burnt-out Records Room. The London Illustrated News. Courtesy the National Library of Canada.

The bell that fell during the fire.

THIS BELL WAS TAKEN FROM THE RUINS
OF THE CLOCK TOWER DESTROYED BY FIRE
FEBRUARY 3, 1916
"THE FIRE RAGED FIERCELY FOR HOURS.
THE MAIN TOWER WAS NOT TOUCHED UNTIL
ABOUT 11 P.M. AND ONE OF THE MOST PATHETIC
INCIDENTS OF THE NIGHT, WHICH MOVED THE
SPECTATORS, WAS THE STRIKING OF THE MID-
NIGHT HOUR BY THE OLD TOWER CLOCK. THERE
SEEMED ALMOST A HUMAN TOUCH AS ITS FAMILIAR
TONES BOOMED OUT FROM THE MASS OF FLAMES"
FROM THE 1916 REPORT OF THE
DEPUTY MINISTER OF PUBLIC WORKS

The inscription with the bell.

The desecrated pile of walls is high above your head. You look upwards because a strange, uncommon noise descends upon your sensitive ear. Outside the wind has risen to anger.... You see a flopping sheet of iron that once was on the roof. It is as big as the poop of a man-of-war. It sways in the breeze lamenting its disquiet as it swings. It is trying to come down to hide from your eyes all that is left of the Canadian House of Commons.

Artifacts from the old Parliament Building still remain in Ottawa and environs. In the Bytown Museum can be found hands of the tower clock, a flag saved by a Dr. Renaud and a bronze statuette. Mounted behind the present Parliament Building complex, as a memento of the fire, is the bell that crashed at the last stroke of midnight on the night of the fire.

At Kingsmere, the estate of the late William Lyon Mackenzie King, Prime Minister of Canada for many years, stones saved from the walls of the old Parliament Building form part of the "Abbey Ruins," a collection of architectural items from Ontario and Québec. Mr. King discovered the stones in an old warehouse and lot on Lyon Street, Ottawa. The Prime Minister received permission from the Department of Public Works to remove some of them and in 1937 he had them built into the "East Wall." In this wall was incorporated the coat of arms of England from Westminster, given to him early in the 1930s. As indicated by his diaries, the coat of arms encased in a wall made of old Parliament Building stones symbolized to him a link between Canada and Great Britain. The "North Wall" also contains stones from the burned Parliament Building. A fireplace, thought to have come from Room 16, is embedded in the lower part of the wall.

One of the walls at Kingsmere that contains stones from the old Parliament Building.
Courtesy the National Capital Commission.

House of Commons opening in the Museum. Prime Minister Borden is at the desk at the left. Arthur Beauchesne is at the left at the Clerk's table. Sir Wilfrid Laurier is at the desk at the right (1918).

Courtesy National Archives Canada, PA 139684.

Chapter 4 — BUSINESS AS USUAL

After the fire there was an immediate need for Parliament to continue to function. In addition to the governing of Canada, three vital issues demanded attention: the war; the cause of the fire in the Parliament Building; and plans for rebuilding the Parliament Building.

At 11 p.m. on the night of the fire, the Prime Minister, Sir Robert Borden, held a unique Cabinet meeting in the room of the Hon. Robert Rogers, who made the Chateau Laurier his home when Parliament was in session. (In *Robert Laird Borden: His Memoirs*, the meeting is mistakenly said to have taken place in the room of the Hon. J.D. Hazen.) The Hon. Hazen, the Hon. Rogers, the Hon. Reid and Mr. Clark were among those present. The Prime Minister presided. They discussed the urgency of finding temporary quarters and several locations were considered, including the new Customs House, the Railway Commissioner's courtroom and the Victoria Memorial Museum. Many other locations were offered, among them Lisgar Collegiate Institute and the Dominion Theatre. The decision was confirmed at 11 a.m., February 4, that the Victoria Memorial Museum would be the Canadian Parliament's new temporary home.

The Minister of Public Works, together with the members of the Internal Economy Commission of the House of Commons, acted as a subcommittee of the Council for the purpose of making all the necessary arrangements. Within 15 hours, the Victoria Memorial Museum was ready for the business of the House of Commons and the Senate to proceed. This was considered by the Prime Minister to be an achievement which reflected great credit upon the Minister of Public Works and his officers. The newspapers described the interior of Parliament's temporary quarters. The few pieces of furniture saved from the fire were used. The massive chair of the Speaker of the Senate was placed on the stage of the auditorium for the Speaker of the House of Commons. The stage was draped in flags and carpeted. Seats were arranged in the body of the hall for members and a desk was provided for the Prime Minister and the Leader of the Opposition. There were rooms for some officials of each House, but members of Parliament had no offices.

The Senate was accommodated in a room that had housed fossils and extinct leviathans. According to *The Globe,* it was a "point which did not escape the notice of certain humourists who see in this arrangement, the hand of political fate."

In the afternoon of 4 February 1916, a procession of ministers and members, in big robe-filled sleighs with many bells, arrived at the Museum. As 3 p.m. approached, the members of Parliament stood around waiting for the opening bell, but there was no bell. Instead, the Sergeant-at-Arms shouldered the mace saved from the Senate Chamber and walked into the Museum theatre followed by Speaker Sévigny. Instead of his customary black silk robes and three-cornered hat, the Speaker wore a borrowed tweed suit and no hat at all. The members took their places and a large crowd of spectators thronged to the gallery surrounding the auditorium.

The Prime Minister, speaking with great feeling, referred to those who had perished and to his own rescue. He said that "the members of the House will have to put up with certain inconveniences in proceeding with the public business...but I believe it will stand out as a good example of the Canadian spirit of determination...."

Messages of sympathy for Canada's great loss were read. These messages continued to arrive for many days. On February 4, the message from His Majesty King George V was received by His Royal Highness the Duke of Connaught, Governor General.

A message of sympathy sent to the Prime Minister from the Governor General was also read in the House. Other messages read on February 4 were from the acting Premier of Saskatchewan, the "Prime Minister" of Québec and the Leader of the Opposition, the Duke and Duchess of Argyle, the Marquis of Landsdowne, the Lord and Lady Aberdeen, the Lieutenant-Governor of Ontario, the Lord Bishop of Toronto, and the Colonial Secretary to the Governor General (signed Bonar Law).*

Parliament sat for 35 minutes on February 4.

On February 8, Parliament convened at 3 p.m. Deputy Rhodes was in the Chair, as Speaker Sévigny had gone to Québec to attend the funerals of Mme Bray and Mme Morin. All in attendance laboured under deep feelings, as before them sat the empty chair of Mr. B.B. Law, who had lost his life in the fire. According to *The Globe*, the Deputy Speaker came to a dramatic halt when, calling the questions on the order paper, he unexpectedly came to three bearing the name of Mr. Law.

Although the location of the Victoria

Memorial Museum, a mile away from departmental buildings, was inconvenient, Parliament continued to sit there until February 1920.

The Senate mace used during this period now replaces the new mace in the House of Commons for one day every year, on February 3, to remind the members of Parliament of the great fire of 1916.

Message of sympathy from King George V.
Courtesy National Archives Canada.

*See Appendix D for further names.

52

The Senate Chamber in the Victoria Memorial Museum.
Courtesy National Archives Canada, C 22916.

Victoria Memorial Museum, temporary home of Canada's Parliament.
Courtesy National Archives Canada, PA 48179.

Is the "Leniency toward alien enemies" policy of the authorities to develop into another case of locking the door after the damage has been done?

"Leniency toward Alien Enemies" the Halifax Herald.
Courtesy the National Library of Canada.

Chapter 5 — PLACING THE BLAME

All of the people of Canada were appalled and incensed at the destruction of their Parliament Building and the governments of the world sympathized. The first concern was whether the origin of the fire had been accidental or incendiary. Officials, members of Parliament and the public remained divided in their opinions throughout and after the investigation.

Even a supernatural force was blamed by a few people. Before the fire, newspapers had reported that the eclipse of the sun, to take place on February 3, "will be visible generally in North America as a partial one only and will (have) a terrible effect on the administration and government heads in every part of the country." (The Ottawa *Evening Journal*).

Because Canada was at war, it was initially believed that the Germans were responsible. Headlines of "Hun Treachery" appeared in the newspapers. The London *Times* wrote of the fire as a "wicked and senseless outrage that can only still harden the indomitable determination of the Canadian people to see war through." Even Sir Wilfrid Laurier was reminded of war. Addressing Parliament on February 4, he stated that the mass of ruins on the Hill reminded him of Louvain and of Rheims, but he also said that the fire was more likely to have been accidental. In addition, he vowed that, if it was found that the fire was incendiary in origin, "we would go on with our work and do everything to bring these cruel murderers to justice." Prime Minister Borden realized that the "public believed that the fire was maliciously set by the enemy—repugnant, but could not be brushed aside as unbelievable."

Further credence to the theory that the fire was the work of the enemy was added by reports in the newspapers. Editor John A. Rathom of *The Journal* in Providence, Rhode Island, had published a warning three weeks before that there was a plot to destroy the Canadian Parliament Building, the home of the Governor General and a Canadian munitions plant. He had warned the U.S. Department of Justice, but no warning had reached Ottawa. The editor would not name his source of information but said that it came from an employee of the German Embassy.

A number of derogatory "cartoons" appeared in the Canadian newspapers.

Concerning the possibility of German involvement, questions arose in Parliament about four men of German origin who held positions of trust in the Dominion Civil Service. Persons of German parentage and those that were born in Germany were required to report periodically to the Dominion police in the East Block, some just because they happened to have German names. Sir Sam Hughes, Minister of Militia and Defence, maintained that the fire was accidental and was incensed by the "wild rumours of German plots, incendiary or otherwise, floating around the Capital" (*Quebec Chronicle*). He vigorously championed the loyalty and good faith of Canadian citizens of German extraction, expressing the hope that in a few days people would return to their "normal state of mind." The Minister of the Militia pointed out that "about 38 German Canadians have already been killed while fighting with the Canadian forces...Captain Hahn of Stratford, the chief intelligence officer with the Canadian Contingent, (regarding whose position there had been much criticism), is now on the firing line where he has already won his D.S.O."

However, Fire Chief Graham insisted that the "fire was set and well set" and other members of Parliament who saw the fire in its early stages, such as Médéric Martin, J.D. Hazen and A.K. Maclean, agreed with him. Others were equally adamant that "Canada's National Disaster" started accidentally. Among these people was the Chief Commissioner of Dominion Police, Colonel A. Percy Sherwood, who maintained that the fire "started right under the nose of a policeman." He claimed that it would have been impossible for a stranger to slip past seven constables and a plainclothes man.

However, once the suspicion of arson had been mentioned, persons in the Parliament Building on 3 February 1916 immediately remembered seeing a variety of suspicious characters. E.M. Macdonald had seen a "suspicious-looking foreigner during the dinner recess who seemed nervous and was pacing up and down." W.B. Northrup saw a stranger in the corridor near the Reading Room. The "stranger" was described on one occasion as wearing checkered clothing and on another occasion a black coat. No stranger was seen by any policeman on the premises. The "spy" thought to have turned off the lights during the fire was, in fact, a tripped electrical switch, one of a number that would shut off the power before the fuse could burn out in case of a short circuit. Fred Wilson was able to turn the lights back on when he reached the electrical board.

Speaker Sévigny said a man who "was speaking French, but thought to be a German" had come to see him the day before the fire desiring access to the building to take photographs.

The request was refused. However, the man, Jules Verlier, a Montreal photographer, was taken into custody on February 4 on suspicion of taking pictures of the fire and buildings for a German agency. He was released an hour later. Two years before, he had taken photographs of the Parliament Buildings, and on February 3 was in the building searching for a friend. Police were satisfied that he had nothing to do with the fire.

Another man suspected of complicity in the burning of the building and detained by the police was Charles Strony, a 28-year-old Belgian pianist. Strony had left Ottawa hurriedly on the night of February 3 by C.P. train. Police Chief Percy Sherwood phoned the Windsor police and Strony was arrested at the Michigan Central tunnel by Provincial Officer James P. Smith who, with Charles Kepkins, Chief of Pinkerton Detective Agency, examined the passengers and found Strony in the parlour car.

Strony, who was the pianist for Madam Edvina, had given a concert for the Governor General and members of his staff on the afternoon of February 3. In the evening he had played in the Russell Theatre from 7:45 p.m. and at the concert's conclusion had to leave quickly for another engagement. He was released the next day and the only item connecting him with the Parliament Building was a postcard of the buildings that he had in his possession.

Another person implicated in the fire was not arrested. A trunk had been left at the Chateau Laurier by a man named Schueiber, who had departed in a hurry sometime before without paying his bill in full. When he sent for his trunk, the police were called in to open it. In it, they found correspondence in German, maps and plans of the Parliament Buildings and other Canadian public buildings. The trunk was then seized by the police.

Subsequent to the fire, the Ottawa Fire Department filed a report detailing their involvement. (See Appendix B.)

A Royal Commission Inquiry was set up to investigate the origin of the fire. Robert A. Pringle, K.C., and Judge D.B. MacTavish (Carleton County Court) were appointed to conduct the inquiry, and W.R. White, K.C., of Pembroke, Ontario, examined the witnesses. The inquiry began on Thursday, February 10 at the City Hall and was concluded on February 24. A report was presented to the Governor General by the Commission on 15 May 1916.

During the inquiry, it became apparent that much had been done to make the building safe from fire and espionage. Guards were stationed at each of the doors and in the corridors with orders to evict strangers. There was also a plain-clothes man in the building.

Fire Chief Graham had suggested locations for hydrants and these had been installed. For further protection, there were 12 pyrene extinguishers, 62 chemical extinguishers, 12 fire reels with 3,150 feet of hose in 100-foot lengths, and one hose reel of 400 feet for emergencies. Also, there were fire axes and other firefighting appliances, and the staff was trained in the use of the equipment. During the fire, the extinguisher used by Constable Moore was in good working order and investigation showed that neither it nor any of the extinguishers had been tampered with. They had been recharged on the 28 and 29 of December 1915. The hydrants were in perfect order, with the exception of one that was frozen but thawed quickly. Twenty streams of water were played on the fire and the pressure was excellent.

As early as 1878, a fire bell had been installed in the tower of the Parliament Building to be used as a fire alarm. It was this bell that crashed through the flames at midnight and now stands behind the Parliament Building as a memento of the fire. (see page 48).

Several years before the fire, a May-Oatway automatic fire alarm system was installed. It was connected to the city fire alarm system and worked perfectly. At the time it was installed, wooden beams in the attic over the Senate and the House of Commons were given a fire-resistant treatment. A 6-horsepower steam engine pump drew water from the river to a reservoir located at the top of one of the towers, from where gravity distributed running water to each office. Water from this reservoir might also help in the event of a fire.

Nevertheless, the building burned with unusual rapidity, creating volumes of dense smoke. It was realized during the investigation that much of the wood in the interior of the building was dry white pine. In addition, the panelling had been richly varnished. The wood floors were recently shellacked and had been treated with a layer of oiled substance to keep down the dust. The Reading Room was covered by a rubber-type matting, which would create volumes of black smoke as it burned.

However, there were no fire checks or iron doors which might have contained the fire, except between the building and the Library. Also, a sprinkling system, which might have repressed the fire, had not been considered feasible, according to Mr. Ewart, consulting architect and formerly Chief Architect for the Department of Public Works. He did admit that it might have been put in the Reading Room. J.B. Hunter,

Deputy Minister of the Department of Public Works, said that they were afraid a sprinkler system might go out of order and some "Member of Parliament might get a shower bath. Then the sprinklers would have gone out quicker than they came in."

Although there were a number of fire escapes, there were too few to service much of the building. Consequently, many areas could only be evacuated when ladders were run up. During the fire, several persons nearly suffocated while awaiting assistance.

It is possible that the deaths of Mme Bray and Mme Morin could have been prevented if easy access to the fire escape through the windows had been assured. Previously, Mme Sévigny had needed help from the Speaker's steward, A.E. Harman, to raise the newly painted windows. Blood was found on the broken glass and curtains of one of the windows and cuts on the hands of the ladies verified their desperate efforts to escape. About 4:30 a.m. on February 4, Mr. Harman and M. Sévigny reached the apartment by way of the fire escape to recover the jewellery and money of Mme Sévigny.

A letter is on file from Robert C. Dunbar, Recording Secretary at the inquest of Mme Morin, to Mr. J.B. Hunter, Deputy Minister of the Department of Public Works. In it, Dunbar enclosed an excerpt from the Coroner's charge which was not included in the report. It concerned the testimony that the doors apparently opened inward. Dunbar repressed this statement "in order to save the Public Works Department from annihilation."

It was also concluded in the investigation that one of the great factors that accelerated the speed with which the fire burned was the ven-tilating system in the building. Thomas Wensley, chief engineer in charge of heating and ventilation, testified that there were two ventilators run by fans in the House of Commons. In the Reading Room, there was a fan in the centre of the floor drawing out air. Pure air came into the room through the doors. This created a very strong current of air in both rooms. Open doors into the corridors produced strong drafts which would cause the flames to race along the ceilings and upper part of the corridors. Heavy varnish on lockers and walls of the corridors fed the flames. Examination of the burned corridors revealed that the fire proceeded, merely burning off the varnish until it reached a wall that blocked the flame sufficiently to have the wood ignite. The fire passed through so rapidly that the lower part of the lockers was still intact and several pairs of over-shoes were found in perfect condition.

A difficult situation existed with regard to the accountability for the safety of the Parliament Buildings. Responsibility was divided between Fire Chief J. Graham and the Commissioner of the Dominion Police Force, P. Sherwood. The Deputy Minister of Public Works, Mr. Hunter, agreed with the police that the government had its own organization for fire protection, and he felt that 75 policemen were capable of detecting and fighting any fire. Fire Chief Graham complained that the firemen had little knowledge of the buildings and he had repeatedly asked that they be inspected by the fire department. Inspector Giroux, in charge of fire protection of government buildings, said he and his five men made daily inspections. The dissension, however, certainly was not evident in the manner in which the firemen and the policemen performed their duty on the night of the fire.

The matter of explosions was also another area of divided opinions. Evidence given during the investigation revealed that Fire Chief Graham and several members of Parliament were convinced that they had heard explosions during the course of the fire. Members of the police force and of the 77th Battalion were equally sure that there were no explosions. There were loud noises, but it was suggested that these noises occurred when flammable gases from shellac and varnish ignited. When sprayed with water, the large globes of the chandeliers burst, making loud reports. Also, there were thundering crashes when the chandelier, ceilings and walls fell during the night. Mr. Knox suggested that perhaps the series of "short reports" he had heard were made by exploding bottles in the liquor room of the Parliamentary Restaurant. No evidence of explosions was found during a thorough examination of the ruins by John A. Pearson, one of the architects selected for rebuilding the Parliament Building.

However, during the investigation, there was complete agreement and great concern by all over the matter of smoking in the Reading Room and other places where so much combustible material was kept. While it was fairly well established that no one had been smoking in the Reading Room on the evening of February 3, it was known that members of Parliament did smoke there. The curator, Stanley Spencer, acknowledged that, while smoking was forbidden to others, the staff found it embarrassing to stop a member from smoking. Mr. Spencer had assisted a member in putting out a fire started by his cigar several weeks before the fire. W.G. Weichel declared that he, with the help of several other members, had put out a small fire only two days before the Parliament Building burned. It was also established that the wastepaper baskets were emptied each day in the morning and therefore would contain combustible material that could have been smouldering for some time during the night of the fire.

In order to identify the nature of the flames that spread so quickly on February 3, an experiment was conducted before Mr. Glass and the investigating committee. Edgar Stansfield, a chemist with the Fuel Testing Division of the Mines Branch, covered a table with asbestos and fires were started on newspapers by ordinary matches, by lighted cigarettes, by lighted cigars and by chemicals which caused materials to burst into flames spontaneously after periods varying from a minute to over an hour. Although chemicals produced a fire more difficult to extinguish, no chemically-induced flame could occur without a pronounced and distinctive odour. No unusual odour had been detected by Mr. Glass on the night of the fire. A match also produced a persistent flame, but in the test, the cigar and cigarette caused newspapers to smoulder but they did not ignite.

When the evidence presented during the investigation was compiled and studied, there was tentative agreement, if no further evidence arrived, that the fire had been accidental. Col. Robert S. Low, a well-known contractor from Halifax, was called in to inspect the ruins. He concluded that, "In the rapid spread of the fire, the system of ventilation combined with extensive varnishing and profuse use of shellac on the floors and woodwork which was the dryest kind of pine, together with loose newspapers (was) the most perfect arrangement ever devised for a sudden and successful conflagration."

The Royal Commission filed a report on 16 May

1916. In their conclusion they reported that "we are of the opinion that all proper precautions were taken to guard against the spread of the fire." They believed that "the ventilating system ...and the air coming in through the doors...had the effect of creating a very strong current which caused the rapid spread of fire in the Reading Room...There is nothing in the evidence to justify your Commissioners in finding that the fire was maliciously set...Commissioners feel very strongly that it might be possible at a later date to obtain evidence (which they cannot reach at the present time), which might establish beyond question whether this fire was incendiary or accidental, and...suggest that this report be treated not as a final report but as an interim report." No further report was tabled.

In his biography, Prime Minister Borden commented on the interim report: there was "nothing in the evidence to justify the Commissioners in finding that the fire was maliciously set...some careless person, throwing a lighted match or cigar into a wastepaper basket and leaving the room (is possible). Flames leaping from the basket quickly reaching the wall which was like tinder and the building was doomed."

One of the immediate responses by Canadians to the destruction of the Parliament Building was increased enlistment in the armed forces. Also more guards were hired to protect all government buildings. All buildings were to have adequate fire escapes and fire doors. The Dominion Fire Commissioner's Office was established in direct response to the fire. Although the last federal election had been in 1911, it was considered expedient for the Liberals and Conservatives to put away all thoughts of an immediate election and deal with the vital issues of the war and of the reconstruction of the Parliament Building. Their important job was the governing of Canada.

In the years following the 1916 fire, many people presented claims for personal losses incurred. In 1918, M. Lemieux told Parliament that "the government had refused to accede to demands which were nothing less than scandalous." However, certain claims from employees were considered justified on equitable or compassionate grounds, and a special committee put aside a sum of $3,500 from which to pay these claims.

In the fire of 3 February 1916, the Library of Parliament was saved through the valiant efforts of firemen and staff. However, it was obvious that it would have to be fireproofed as quickly as possible. In spite of many improvements (1916 to 1920) to prevent future fire damage, a fire broke out on 4 August 1952 in the Library roof and, in extinguishing it, water damage was extensive. To prevent this situation from recurring, $2 million were spent over a period of four years to reconstruct the entire interior of the Library from subbasement to roof. Fire-resistant materials were used, but great care was taken to preserve the original beauty of the woodwork. The Library of Parliament was reopened in 1956.

Chapter 6 — THE RECONSTRUCTION

The Rt. Hon. Sir Robert Borden, in the Halifax *Herald*, predicted about the new building, "ever a grander pile will rise, Phoenix-like from the ashes of that which is today blackened smouldering ruin." It was agreed by all that the new building would be built in Gothic style to harmonize with the existing East and West blocks.

Well-known architects John A. Pearson from Toronto and J.D. Marchand from Québec were immediately appointed by the Hon. Robert Rogers to inspect the ruins and to work on plans for the new building. Robert S. Low, a contractor in the Maritime Provinces, was also called in to inspect the ruins. Mr. David Ewart of the Department of Public Works was consulting architect.

On 14 February 1916, after the recovery by firemen of four of the five bodies that were buried in the debris, the work of removing the wreckage was taken over from the Parliamentary staff by P. Lyall and Sons Construction Company. Although this company was formally engaged on May 14 to construct the new building, a contract mutually agreeable to them and to the government was not signed until September. On May 16, Pearson and Marchand were officially hired to prepare plans and to oversee the construction.

It was decided by Parliament that a Joint Committee be appointed to deal with the many details of the reconstruction of the Parliament Building and to work closely with architects and the construction company. Prime Minister Borden and the Leader of the Opposition, the Rt. Hon. Sir Wilfrid Laurier, each nominated four members from their respective parties. The Hon. Robert Rogers, Minister of Public Works, acted as chairman. With the committee representing both political parties, patronage should be eliminated and the purchase of materials and the employment of labour should be free from political influence and considerations. The Deputy Minister of Public Works, Mr. Hunter, stated, "This is the first time in the history of Canada that an attempt has been made to construct a large monumental public work with the co-operation of both political parties...Labours of the committee have been most harmonious to that end."

The committee was appointed on April 24 and the official announcement was made on 8 May 1916. The Joint Parliamentary Committee was made up of the following Members:. Hon. James Reid, Hon. J.D. Hazen, Senator Sir James Lougheed, Hon. P.E. Blondin, Hon. R. Lemieux, Hon. Charles Murphy, Hon. William Pugsley, Senator R. Watson.* Their first meeting took place on 9 May 1916.

Discussed in Parliament was the need for the new building to have increased accommodation for the members of Parliament representing a growing Canada. Even before the fire, the Centre Block was becoming crowded as new provinces joined the Dominion. The House of Commons Chamber, in particular, was too small. After the viewing of the plans proposed for the new building on March 21, it became apparent to the members and to the committee that in order to have the required space for offices and other functions, an additional storey was needed. A sketch

*See Appendix C.

with the additional storey was adopted on 15 May 1916. It did not materially interfere with the exterior design.

A February 17 architects' report stating that the walls standing after the fire could be used proved overoptimistic. Many of the limestone blocks were impaired by the intense heat and the mortar had cracked in many places. The stone layers of the wall had separated. Certainly, the old wall could not support an additional storey.

There was much criticism by some of the members of Parliament and the press against the decision to tear down the walls left standing after the fire. Questions were asked as to why these walls were not incorporated into the new building. Many thought that the decision had been taken and acted upon in haste without proper discussion and consideration of the implications associated with such a decision.

As early as 23 May 1916, Deputy Minister Hunter had complained in a telegram to Mr. Pearson about the manner in which the two shifts of wrecking crews were handling the stone. On June 20, he requested details of the arrangements that were being carried out to mark the stone that was being taken down to be stored. As no answer was forthcoming, on June 27 he requested an immediate answer to "what portion of the walls is to be left intact and what portion is...to be taken down carefully for the purpose of reusing."

By late July the entire walls and floors of the old Parliament Building were taken down and the debris was being cleared from the site in preparation for rebuilding.

It was not until July 29 that the Hon. R. Rogers received a long report from architects Pearson and Marchand to explain reasons for demolishing the walls, which by this time were torn down. The committee did not meet until the 3rd and 4th of August and until then had not had the opportunity to discuss the need to remove all the walls and the new (1912) West Wing. Eventually, the architects acknowledged that the decision to demolish had been entirely theirs. Sir Wilfrid Laurier and many members of Parliament were justifiably upset, as the site had been cleared before the committee had been consulted.

Because of the many complaints and derogatory newspaper articles, the committee asked Deputy Minister Hunter to make public the architects' "statement of their proceedings and of the reasons which have induced them to take the course adopted to secure such restoration and reconstruction." The rather lengthy report mentioned the fact that additional accommodation was required, with better lighting and ventilation of the Chambers. The additional storey required must not materially interfere with the exterior design. "Several schemes were plotted endeavouring to retain the West Wing but it was found impossible to get a properly balanced plan. We were convinced that no satisfactory plan could be arrived at by endeavouring to tack a building on to the West Wing.... It also necessitated removal of the tower, which under any circumstances would have had to be almost entirely taken down, owing to the effects of the fire.... Also, placing an extra storey upon the building necessitated the taking down of the top storey of the external walls."

During their inspection of the ruins, the architects discovered many defects therein. "It was found that in numerous places the backing and interior masonry of the walls...revealed a very shocking state of affairs. The outer stone masonry

had not been bonded into the inner backing, and in many places there were voids in the walls from four to eight inches wide and the full height and width of the piers between the windows.... It was necessary to follow down and take out this defective masonry with the result that portions of the south wall and end pavilions...have had to be taken down to the level of the outer walls with a straight joint and in no way (were they) tied to the outer walls. The mortar in which the brick and stone had been laid was of a very poor quality, in some cases there was little or no lime used and certain walls in the foundations had the centre filled with dry rubble...more markedly noticeable in the lower portions of the tower and south centre walls extending east and west from the tower to the East and West Pavilions. There was serious settlement in the tower, evidenced by the number of stones in the weatherings that had been cut out and replaced at a later date.... The decision to have an additional storey made it necessary to both widen and heighten the tower which required it to be taken down in any event.... To avoid future danger to fire, it would be desirable to remove the boiler house for light, heat and power purposes to outside the building which necessitated removal of former heating and ventilating plants, chimney stack and boiler room."

Wall showing poor anchoring of interior walls and piers, 7 July 1916.

Courtesy National Archives of Canada, PA 89055.

63

To the press it was reported that "the committee, after careful consideration, have no hesitation, upon the evidence on which was based the removal of the walls by the architects, in agreeing with them that the taking down of the walls was absolutely necessary. In view of their dangerous condition, to have attempted to utilize them would, in the opinion of the committee, have been wholly unjustifiable.... The committee have given directions that the stone which has been removed from the walls...shall be utilized as much as possible in the reconstruction."

The poor condition of the original walls was further confirmed in late summer by Henry Holgate, consulting engineer of Montreal. He stated that "the fire, of course, affected them, but the system of construction of the masonry was such as must be generally condemned, and I can see no justification in using the old walls, owing to their being radically bad and unsafe, more especially if they had to carry another floor."

The walls were taken down without formal approval of the Joint Parliamentary Committee, but certainly the condition of the walls and their need to be demolished had been well publicized. On July 7, the Ottawa *Free Press* printed an article under the heading "Tower on Hill in Danger of Collapse." The Hon. Robert Rogers had met with the newspapermen for the purpose of viewing the old walls to see why they would have to be removed. Stones that had cracked and split due to the strain of the weight of the tower had been poorly patched and looked as if they would collapse under the weight of the tower. "Now, gentlemen, you see why the Parliamentary Committee which is co-operating with me in this work decided that all the old walls had to come down." This statement may have been a month pre-

mature, but the committee did eventually agree completely with the decision.

Mr. Lyall pointed out to them that one corner of the building had been built on earth instead of rock. Had they gone another eight inches lower they would have reached rock. "We have some job pulling (the new West Wing) down, but the rest of the building falls down. For everything that is being done, we have the unanimous approval of the Parliamentary Committee.... We intend to make a good job of it and there will be no graft if we can help it."

The same day that the article appeared in the Ottawa *Free Press* (7 July 1916), photographs were taken of many of the defects found in the walls and they are in the archival records of the Department of Public Works.

During the demolition, scaffolding was built along the entire front of the old walls at a cost of $9,954.04. Later, part of the scaffolding was sold to the Military Hospital Commission for $553.73 and the remainder was used for shoring and bracing in the construction of the new building.

For the construction, as with the original building, the Nepean quarry supplied the blocks of stone. Interior corridors and stairways were built of Tyndall stone quarried in Manitoba, and Ohio sandstone was used for dressings, gablets and pinnacles. However, the use of contrasting red sandstone for window and door trim was overruled by the architects and by the Governor General. Wallace sandstone, not used in the original building, was introduced for courts, air towers, light wells, chimneys and penthouses. Instead of slate from Vermont, used on the original roof, the new roof was copper. Materials entering into the construction of the building were to come from Canada whenever possible.

Reconstruction, 3 August 1916.   Courtesy National Archives Canada, PA 387524.

Reconstruction, 15 August 1916.   Courtesy National Archives Canada, PA 130624.

Although the interior floor plans for the new building were similar to those of the old Centre Block, they eliminated many corridors that had contributed to funneling the fire through the old building. Also, there was to be no sleeping accommodation for the Speakers of the Houses. The Ottawa *Evening Journal* agreed with this controversial decision: "Residential quarters are not necessary. Arrangements for (their) comfort can be provided without turning the structure into a species of boarding house...pink teas in the Parliament Buildings are not essential to the Speaker's dignity." Speakers of both the House of Commons and the Senate have elegant suites of rooms but the apartments have "neither cellar, scullery or bedroom."

Prime Minister Borden was generally pleased with the plans, although he would have preferred private corridors for the Prime Minister and the Leader of the Opposition to enter the Chamber without being "buttonholed and diverted from some urgent matter engaging their attention." He also wished for galleries in the Senate Chamber, but he considered that these disadvantages were offset by the increased accommodation, improvements in the access to light and air, and the improved acoustics of the Chambers. He was especially pleased with the plans for "the great sweep of the Hall of Fame leading to the Library and the beautiful memorial tower."

One of the great concerns in planning the new building was the degree to which it would be fireproof. The Hon. F.B. Carvell, recently appointed Minister of the Department of Public Works, considering the type of construction and the materials, could "not conceive there will be a fire in the new building." However, he added, "That may be a violent assumption! There will

not be a partition of wood of any kind or description excepting the doors and baseboards around the inside of the offices. There will be no door frames as such; there are no wooden window frames or wooden sashes. Everything is either metal or concrete. Therefore, while you might burn the desks and papers in a room...that would be the end of it, so that I am not bothering my head very much about a fire alarm in the new building."

In 1986, some 68 years after the Parliament Hill's Centre Block was rebuilt, concern for the safety of the building again was being voiced. The Ottawa *Citizen* headlined an article "Centre Block Fire Hazard." A study had been prepared by two architectural firms at the request of the Department of Public Works that urged major repairs which would cost $50 million. A complete overhaul of the electrical system with new lighting is needed. Fire sprinklers should be installed in the top four floors. (They have recently been installed in the basement and ground floor.) New fire exits are required and all maintenance work shops should be moved to another building. New heating, ventilation and air conditioning systems are needed. Also, recommendations were made for replacing sections of roofs, repairing windows and restoring exterior stone. This work, expected to take eight or nine years on a floor-to-floor basis, is "needed to preserve the historic landmark for future generations."

In October 1987, the Centre Block was evacuated due to smoke billowing throughout the sixth floor. Speaker John Fraser was quoted in the Ottawa *Citizen* as saying, "...the latest mechanical problem is further proof (of the need) to repair the 68-year old building." The Public Works Minister said that the $7 million first phase

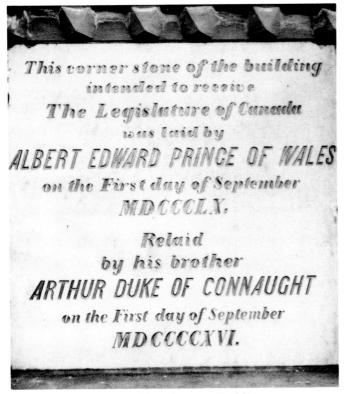

Cornerstone of the Old Parliament Building.
Courtesy National Archives Canada, PA 34435.

of repairs will be finished in the summer of 1988.

In the summer of 1916, during the preparation for the reconstruction of the Parliament Building, plans were made to re-lay the cornerstone of the old building in a ceremony on September 1. The stone was removed from the ruins and cleaned. The cornerstone, originally laid in 1860 by the Prince of Wales (later King Edward VII) was re-laid at the northeast corner of the new building by his brother, the Duke of Connaught, the Governor General of Canada.

In the old cornerstone was a book printed in 1860 about the tour of the Prince of Wales, coins in a glass bottle and a parchment scroll inscribed with the details of the laying of the stone on 1 September 1860. Included in the 1916 cornerstone were: a $10 gold piece and a $5 gold coin dated 1912, first issue of gold coins minted in Canada; the Canadian coins of 1916; die-proofs and Canadian postage stamps; the current daily newspapers of 31 August 1916, the Ottawa *Evening Journal*, the Ottawa *Free Press* and *Le Droit*, and the 1 September 1916 copy of *The Morning Citizen*.

For the rebuilding of the Parliament Building a large work force was required. For example, during the weeks of 29 November to 15 December 1917, exclusive of superintendents and office staff, 706 men were employed.

In May 1916, the estimated cost for the completed building was just over $5 million. There was no help from insurance to cover the cost. The Government of Canada does not carry insurance on its buildings, being of the opinion that over a period of time the premiums would be more than any probable losses. In May 1919, to the consternation of the members of Parliament, the projected cost of the Parliament Building had risen to $8

Reconstruction,
7 August 1918.
Courtesy National
Archives Canada,
C 38764.

million. However, when completed, the final cost to build and furnish the building had escalated to $12,226,582.32. Individual expenses are found in the debates of the House of Commons during the period of construction and in the records of the Department of Public Works.

Throughout this period, Parliament continued to sit at the Victoria Memorial Museum. The members of Parliament were eager to move to their new building and progress was anxiously watched. In September 1919, to an inquiry as to whether the next session could be held at the Hill, the Hon. A.L. Sifton, then Minister of Public Works, replied, "I can hold a wonderful amount of hope, but can give no promises."

Finally the building had progressed to the point that the Fourth Session of the Thirteenth Parliament, opening on 26 February 1920, took place in the new Parliament Building.

However, the building was far from being completed. The tower, which would rise about 200 feet from base to top of the bronze flagstaff, had yet to be finished. In one of the many discussions in Parliament concerning the plans for the main tower, S.W. Jacobs, then Member of Parliament for Montreal-Cartier, requested that "proper provision be made for lodgement of such prisoners as we may have from time to time." The Hon. Carvell's reply that "a room would be fixed up in the basement of the tower for such characters as my Honourable friend described" was considered by Mr. Jacobs as "absolutely unconstitutional! The proper place to put prisoners is in the tower."

The tower was to have a more acceptable purpose. It was decided to make the tower a monument to the service and sacrifice of Canadians in the World War. It became known as the Victory or Peace Tower.

During reconstruction.
Saturday Night,
Toronto.
Courtesy National Archives
Canada.

Parliament Building without Peace Tower. Photo by W.J. Topley.   Courtesy National Archives Canada, PA 12925.

Tower construction, July 1921.
Courtesy National Archives Canada, C 38750.

The cornerstone of the tower was laid on 1 September 1919 by Edward, Prince of Wales (later King Edward VIII). The stone, quarried at Wallace, Nova Scotia, contains a receptacle holding a scroll, coins, postage stamps, newspapers and messages of greeting. From raised dots under certain letters of the words inscribed on the stone, the year of dedication can be ascertained. Once completed, the tower provided space for a memorial chamber commemorating those who died in the wars. It was also a campanile and clock tower.

At Canada's Diamond Jubilee, on 1 July 1927, Prime Minister Mackenzie King dedicated the tower as a memorial to those who died during World War I and to the cause of peace. It is worth noting that the work specified in the original drawings and plans for the reconstruction of the Parliament Building after the 3 February 1916 fire is to date not completed. For example, the carving on the interior has not been finished as yet. In addition, the building has undergone changes and will continue to be subject to changes as need arises and Canada develops.

However, today, as in 1861, the words of English novelist Anthony Trollope ring as true for the present Parliament Building as they did for the original building so cruelly destroyed by fire: "As regards purity of art and manliness of conception the work is entitled to the highest praise. ... I have no hesitation in risking my reputation for judgement in giving my warmest commendation... as regards beauty of outline and truthful nobility of detail... I know no modern Gothic purer of its kind or less sullied with fictitious ornamentation and I know no site for such a set of buildings so happy as regards both beauty and grandeur."

Ceremony marking the Diamond Jubilee of Confederation at Parliament Hill,
1 July 1927.

Photo by E.M. Finn.
Courtesy National Archives Canada, C 18068.

Appendix A
ALPHABETICAL LIST
of the
MEMBERS OF THE HOUSE OF COMMONS
and their Constituencies
Sixth Session, Twelfth Parliament.
1916

Achim, Honoré — Labelle
Alguire, Duncan Orestes — Stormount
Ames, Herbert Brown — Montreal, St. Antoine
Armstrong, J.A. Macdonald — York, Ontario, N.
Armstrong, Joseph E. — Lambton, E.
Arthurs, James — Parry Sound
Baker, George Harold — Brôme
Ball, R.J. — Grey S.
Barnard, George Henry — Victoria, B.C.
Barbette, Joseph Arthur — Berthier
Béland, Hon. Henri Sévérin — Beauce
Bellemare, A. — Maskinongé
Bennett, Richard Bedford — Calgary
Bennett, William H. — Simcoe, E.
Best, John A. — Dufferin
Bickerdike, Robert — Montreal, St. Lawrence
Blain, Richard — Peel
Blondin, Hon. Pierre Edouard — Champlain
Boivin, George Henry — Shefford
Borden, Rt. Hon. Sir Robert Laird — Halifax
Boulay, Herménégilde — Rimouski
Bourassa, J. Boutin — Lévis
Bowman, James — Huron, E.
Boyce, Arthur Cyril — Algoma West
Boyer, Gustave — Vaudreuil
Boys, W. A. — South Simcoe
Brabazon, Gerald H. — Pontiac
Bradbury, George Henry — Selkirk
Bristol, Edmund — Toronto Centre
Broder, Hon. Andrew — Dundas
Brouillard, Ovide — Drummond and Arthabaska
Buchanan, William Ashbury — Medicine Hat
Bureau, Jacques — Three Rivers and St. Maurice

Burnham, John H. — Peterborough, W.
Burrell, Hon. Martin — Yale-Cariboo
Cardin, Pierre Joseph Arthur — Richelieu
Carrick, John James — Thunder Bay and Rainy River
Carroll, W.F. — Cape Breton, South
Carvell, Frank Broadstreet — Carleton, N.B.
Casgrain, Hon. Thomas Chase — Québec County
Cash, Edward L. — Mackenzie
Chabot, John Leo — Ottawa
Champagne, Albert — Battleford
Charlton, William Andrew — Norfolk
Chisholm, Alexander W. — Inverness
Chisholm, William — Antigonish
Clark, Hugh — Bruce, N.
Clark, Michael — Red Deer
Clarke, Alfred Henry — Essex, S.
Clarke, W.A. — Wellington, N.
Clements, Herbert Sylvester — Comox-Atlin
Cochrane, Hon. Francis — Nipissing
Cockshutt, William Foster — Brantford
Copp, Arthur Bliss — Westmorland
Cromwell, Frederick Robert — Compton
Crothers, Hon. Thomas Wilson — Elgin, W.
Cruise, Robert — Dauphin
Currie, John Allister — Simcoe, N.
Davidson, Avard L. — Annapolis
Delisle, Michel Siméon — Portneuf
Demers, Marie Joseph — St. John and Iberville
Descarries, Joseph A. — Jacques Cartier
Devlin, Emmanuel B. — Wright
Doherty, Hon. Charles Joseph — Montreal, St. Anne
Donaldson, Samuel J. — Prince Albert
Douglas, James M. — Strathcona
Edwards, John Wesley — Frontenac
Elliott, George A. — Middlesex, N.
Ethier, Joseph Arthur Calixte — Two Mountains
Fisher, John Henry — Brant
Forget, Sir Rodolphe — Charlevoix & Montmorency
Fortier, Edmond — Lotbinière
Foster, Hon. Sir George Eulas — Toronto North
Fowler, George William — Kings and Albert

Fripp, Alfred Ernest — Ottawa
Gauthier, Louis Joseph — St. Hyacinthe
Gauthier, Louis Philippe — Gaspé
Gauvreau, Charles Arthur — Témiscouata
German, William Manley — Welland
Girard, Joseph — Chicoutimi and Saguenay
Glass, S. Francis — Middlesex, E.
Gordon, David Alexander — Kent, E.
Graham, Hon. George P. — Renfrew, S.
Gray, William — London
Green, R.F. — Kootenay
Guilbault, Joseph Pierre Octave — Joliette
Guthrie, Hugh — Wellington, S.
Hanna, A.E. — Lanark, S.
Hartt, Thomas A. — Charlotte
Hazen, Hon. John Douglas — St. John City and County
Henderson, Hon. David — Halton
Hepburn, Bernard Rickart — Prince Edward
Hughes, James Joseph — Kings, P.E.I.
Hughes, Hon. Sir Sam — Victoria, Ont.
Jameson, Clarence — Digby
Kay, William Frederick — Missisquoi
Kemp, Hon. Albert Edward — Toronto East
Knowles, William Erskine — Moose Jaw
Kyte, George W. — Richmond, N.S.
Lachance, Arthur — Québec Centre
Lafortune, David A. — Montcalm
Lalor, Francis Ramsay — Haldimand
Lamarche, Paul Emile — Nicolet
Lanctôt, Roch — Laprairie-Napierville
Lapointe, Ernest — Kamouraska
Lapointe, Louis A. — Montreal, St. James
Laurier, Rt. Hon. Sir Wilfrid — Québec East, Soulanges
Lavallée, Joseph Octave — Bellechasse
Law, Bowman Brown — Yarmouth
Lemieux, Hon. Rodolphe — Rouville
Lespérance, David Ovide — Montmagny
Lewis, Edward Norman — Huron, W.
Loggie, William Stewart — Northumberland, N.B.
Lovell, Charles Henry — Stanstead

Macdonald, Edward Mortimer — Pictou
Macdonell, Angus Claude — Toronto South
Maclean, Alexander K. — Halifax
Maclean, William Findlay — York, Ontario, S.
MacNutt, Thomas — Saltcoats
McCoig, Archibald Blake — Kent, W.
McCraney, George E. — Saskatoon
McCrea, Francis N. — Sherbrooke
McCurdy, Fleming Blanchard — Shelburne and Queens
McKenzie, Daniel D. — Cape Breton, N.
McLean, Angus A. — Queens, P.E.I.
McLean, Hugh Havelock — Sunbury and Queens
McLeod, Harry F. — York, N.B.
McMillan, John Angus — Glengarry
Marcil, Hon. Charles — Bonaventure
Marcile, Joseph Edmond — Bagot
Marshall, David — Elgin, E.
Martin, Médéric — Montreal, St. Mary's
Martin, William Melville — Regina
Meighen, Hon. Arthur — Portage la Prairie
Merner, Jonathan Joseph — Huron, S.
Michaud, Pius — Victoria, N.B.
Middlebro, William Sora — Grey, N.
Molloy, John Patrick — Provencher
Mondou, A.A. — Yamaska
Morphy, H.B. — Perth, N.
Morris, James — Châteauguay
Morrison, A. — Macdonald
Munson, Charles Arthur — Northumberland, Ont., W.
Murphy, Hon. Charles — Russell
Neely, Davis Bradley — Humboldt
Nesbitt, Edward Walter — Oxford, N.
Nicholson, Donald — Queens, P.E.I.
Nickle, William Folger — Kingston
Northrup, William Barton — Hastings, E.
Oliver, Hon. Frank — Edmonton
Osler, Sir Edmund Boyd — Toronto West
Pacaud, Lucien Turcotte — Mégantic
Papineau, Louis J. — Beauharnois
Paquet, Eugène — L'Islet
Pardee, Frederick Forsyth — Lambton, W.

Patenaude, Hon. E.L. — Hochelaga
Paul, William James — Lennox and Addington
Pelletier, Hon. Louis Philippe — Québec County
Perley, Hon. Sir George Halsey — Argenteuil
Porter, Edward Guss — Hastings, W.
Power, William — Québec West
Proulx, Edmond — Prescott
Pugsley, Hon. William — St. John City
Rainville, Joseph Hormisdas — Chambly and
    Verchères
Reid, James — Restigouche
Reid, Hon. John D. — Grenville
Rhodes, Edgar N. — Cumberland
Robb, James Alexander — Huntingdon
Robidoux, Ferdinand Joseph — Kent, N.B.
Roche, Hon. William James — Marquette
Rochon, Gédéon — Terrebonne
Rogers, Hon. Robert — Winnipeg
Ross, Duncan Campbell — Middlesex, W.
Schaffner, Frederick Laurence — Souris
Scott, Frank Stewart — South Waterloo
Séguin, Paul Arthur — L'Assomption
Sévigny, Albert — Dorchester
Sexsmith, John A. — Peterborough, E.
Sharpe, Samuel — Ontario, N.
Shepherd, Francis Henry — Nanaimo
Sinclair, John H. — Guysborough
Smith, William — Ontario, S.
Smyth, William Ross — Algoma, E.
Stanfield, John — Colchester
Steele, Michael — Perth, S.
Stevens, Henry Herbert — Vancouver
Stewart, Dugald — Lunenburg
Stewart, Thomas Joseph — Hamilton West
Sutherland, Donald — Oxford, S.
Taylor, James Davis — New Westminster
Thoburn, William — Lanark, N.
Thompson, Alfred — Yukon Territory
Thomson, Levy — Qu'Appelle
Thornton, Charles Jonas — Durham
Tobin, Edmund William — Richmond and Wolfe

Tremain, Hadley B. — Hants
Truax, Reuben E. — Bruce, S.
Turgeon, Onésiphore — Gloucester
Turriff, John Gillanders — Assiniboia
Verville, Alphonse — Maisonneuve
Walker, Henry Joseph — Northumberland, Ont., E.
Wallace, Thomas George — York, Ont., Centre
Warnock, David — Macleod
Webster, John — Brockville
Weichel, William George — Waterloo, N.
White, Gerald Verner — Renfrew, N.
White, William Henry — Victoria, Alta.
White, Hon. Sir William Thomas — Leeds
Wilcox, Oliver J. — Essex, N.
Wilson, Charles Avila — Laval
Wilson, Gordon Crooks — Wentworth
Wright, William — Muskoka

**The Canadian Ministry on 3 February 1916
and During the Investigation**

1. The Right Hon. Sir Robert Laird Borden,
G.C.M.G., K.C., First Minister, President of the
Privy Council (10 October 1911).*
2. The Hon. Sir George Eulas Foster, K.C.M.G.,
B.A., D.C.L., LL.D.,Minister of Trade and Commerce
(10 October 1911).
3. The Hon. Sir George Halsey Perley, K.C.M.G.,
B.A., Minister of Overseas Military Forces for
Canada in the United Kingdom (31 October 1916;
originally sworn in as Member of the Cabinet
without Portfolio, 10 October 1911).
4. The Hon. Robert Rogers, Minister of Public
Works (29 October 1912; first sworn in as
Minister of the Interior, 10 October 1911).
5. The Hon. Francis Cochrane, Minister of
Railways and Canals (10 October 1911).
6. The Hon. Sir William Thomas White, K.C.M.G.,
B.A., Minister of Finance (10 October 1911).

7. The Hon. John Douglas Hazen, K.C., B.A., B.C.L., Minister of Marine and Fisheries and Minister of the Naval Services (10 October 1911).

8. The Hon. Charles Joseph Doherty, K.C., D.C.L., LL.D., Minister of Justice (10 October 1911).

9. Major-General The Hon. Sir Sam Hughes, K.C.B., Minister of Militia and Defence (10 October 1911).

10. The Hon. William James Roche, M.D., Minister of the Interior (29 October 1912; first sworn in as Secretary of State, 10 October 1911).

11. The Hon. Thomas Wilson Crothers, K.C., B.A., Minister of Labour (10 October 1911).

12. The Hon. John Dowsley Reid, M.D., Minister of Customs (10 October 1911).

13. The Hon. Albert Edward Kemp, Member of the Cabinet without Portfolio (10 October 1911).

14. The Hon. James Alexander Lougheed, K.C., Senator, Member of the Cabinet without Portfolio (10 October 1911).

15. The Hon. Martin Burrell, Minister of Agriculture (10 October 1911).

16. The Hon. Thomas Chase Casgrain, K.C., Postmaster-General (20 October 1914).

17. The Hon. Pierre Edouard Blondin, Secretary of State of Canada (first sworn in as Minister of Inland Revenue, 20 October 1914; appointed Secretary of State and Minister of Mines, 6 October 1916).

18. The Hon. Arthur Meighen, M.A., K.C., Solicitor-General (assumed office as such 30 September 1915).

19. The Hon. Esioff-Léon Patenaude, K.C., Minister of Inland Revenue (6 October 1915).

*Dates within parentheses denote dates of appointment

APPENDIX B
Ottawa Fire Department Report

District No.: Western
Box: No. 255 and Second Alarm. Day: Thursday.
Date: Feb. 3, 1916.
Time received 8:57 and 9:05 o'clock p.m., by gong.
Street: Parliament Hill. Ward: Victoria.
Description of building, storeys: 3 and 4.
Material: stone.
Occupied by: Dominion Government as Parliament Buildings.
Owner: Dominion Government.

Fire originated on: First floor; reading-room.
Caused by: First noticed at desk among some newspapers.
Fire extended: Practically throughout building.
Hydrant was located: All hydrants except one on Parliament Hill, and one on Wellington Street.
Served by engines: Nos. 2, 3, 4, 7, 8, 9, and Relief engine and Hull engine.
Number of streams laid: 20
Length of hose in feet: 11,800.
Extinguished with: Fourteen engine pipe-streams and two deluge streams of three lines apiece.
Returned quarters: Fire under control at 2 o'clock a.m.
Ladders used: 861 feet.
Services of salvage: 18 salvage covers.
Services of steam engine: No. 4 worked 22 hours; No. 7 worked 27 hours; No. 9 worked 24 hours; Relief engine worked 22 hours; Hull engine worked 12 hours.
Services of motor engines: No. 2 worked 25 hours; No. 3 worked 22 hours; No. 8 worked 23 hours.

APPENDIX C
The Joint Parliamentary Committee
1916–1921

Only 2 members served on the committee for the 5 years, Senator Lougheed and Senator Watson. A succession of ministers of the Department of Public Works chaired the meetings:

Hon. R. Rogers resigned on 22 August and was succeeded by
Hon. F.B. Carvell who was appointed Minister on 3 October 1917 and resigned on 2 August 1919 and was succeeded by
Hon. A.L. Sifton, appointed Minister on 3 September 1919 and resigned on 31 December 1919 and was succeeded by
Hon. Dr. Reid as Minister on 31 December 1919. He was succeeded as Minister by
Hon. F.B. McCurdy, appointed Minister on 31 July 1920.

Among the Members of Parliament:
Hon. Charles Murphy resigned on 24 June 1916. He never acted because of illness. He was not replaced.
Hon. R. Lemieux resigned on 1 September 1916 after a disagreement about contracts. He was not replaced.
Hon. J.D. Hazen retired as Minister of the Marine on 3 October 1917 and was replaced by Hon. C.C. Ballantyne on 24 October.
Hon. P.E. Blondin left for overseas Military Service on 7 October 1917 and was replaced by Hon. G.D. Robertson on 25 March 1919.
Hon. Wm. Pugsley resigned on 23 February 1918 and was replaced by Hon. J.A. Calder on 25 March 1919.

Hon. J.A. Stewart and Hon. R. Monty were nominated by the Right Honourable Arthur Meighen on 22 September 1921 to replace Hon. Dr. Reid and Hon. J.A. Calder who were elevated to the Senate.

A weekly report of progress was sent to each of the committee members by the architects. By October 1921, about 64 meetings had taken place.

APPENDIX D

For a number of days, messages of condolences were read to the Members of Parliament. During this time messages were received from: House of Assembly, Barbados; Council of the City of Hull; Secretary of State of the U.S.A.; Governor of Japan; Barbados Chamber of Commerce; Vancouver Canadian Japanese Association; Prime Minister of New Zealand; Governor General of Australia; Lord Kitchener; Governor of Newfoundland; Premiers of the Canadian Provinces; French, Russian and Italian Consuls; Governor and People of South Africa; President of the Chamber of Deputies; Empire Parliamentary Association; French Senate; Lord and Lady Grey; Royal Colonial Institute; John S. Hendrie; Government and People of Newfoundland; Metropolitan Club, New York; Mayor of Montreal; Sir George Perley; Bishop of Toronto; Grand Trunk Board; Ireland; Alexander of Teck; Canadian Club of Boston; Canadian Corps; Salvation Army; Belgian Government; Swedish Government; Rabbi Jacobs, Toronto; Norwegian Government; the French House of Deputies, France; Legislative Assembly of the Province of Québec; Empire Parliamentary Association, London, England; Lord Willingdon, Governor, on behalf of the Bombay Presidency, Rajkot, India.

SOURCES OF INFORMATION

National Archives Canada
The National Library of Canada
Bibliothèque nationale du Québec
National Capital Commission
Archives of the City of Ottawa

BIBLIOGRAPHY

Borden, R.L. *Robert Laird Borden: His Memoirs.* London, 1938.
Edgar, Hon. J.D. *Canada and its Capital.* Toronto, 1898.
Eggleston, W. *The Queen's Choice.* Ottawa, 1961.
The National Film Board of Canada. *Canada's Houses of Parliament.* 1967.
Woods, S. *Ottawa: The Capital of Canada.* Toronto, 1980.

INDEX

F. Varkaris

LUCILE FINSTEN (née Dugas) is a Franco-Ontarian and a native of Ottawa. She is a graduate of the University of Ottawa with a degree in Linguistics and Literature.

After many years as a personnel administrator in the Federal Public Service in Ottawa, Lucile now works as a management consultant.

JANE VARKARIS studied at the University of Toronto where she received her Bachelor and Master of Arts degrees.

Since moving to Ottawa over thirty years ago, she has devoted much time to researching various areas of Canadiana and already has to her credit, three books on horology. In addition, she has contributed material on clocks and watches to a number of books and publications both in North America and Europe.

Her contribution to Canadian horology earned her recognition as a Fellow of the National Association of Watch and Clock Collectors and the Award of Merit was presented to her by Chapter 111 of the NAWCC of which she is a founding member.

Books by Jane and Costas Varkaris:

Nathan Fellows Dupuis, Professor and Clockmaker of Queen's University and His Family
The Pequegnat Story, The Family and the Clocks

Book by Jane Varkaris and James E. Connell:
The Canada and Hamilton Clock Companies

F. Varkaris